Further Praise

"Finally there is a book written for men, by a man, that gets right to the heart of our struggles with a clear pathway towards emotional freedom."—**Mike Robbins, author of** *Be Yourself, Everyone Else Is Already Taken*

"Ray Arata masterfully presents to the reader a much needed authentic tough love: tough love of the man for himself, tough love from other men, tough love from the woman. This book is truly a must read for today's man on his path to be truly authentic in his roles as husband, father, leader, and friend."—**Lee Glickstein, Founder and President, Speaking Circles International**

"*Wake Up, Man Up, Step Up* is not a book about discovering a guru or a god and following; it is a book that requires you to discover yourself and lead. It is not a book you read; it is a book that invites you to participate in rewriting the book others have written for you. In brief, *Wake Up, Man Up, Step Up* doesn't let you 'get away' with reading *about* men; it requires you to be a man."—**Warren Farrell, Ph.D., author of** *Why Men Are the Way They Are* **and** *The Myth of Male Power*

"More than a dozen years after getting the 'wake-up call' that began his men's journey, Ray Arata has penned a book to guide his brethren—should they take up his challenge to join him. This book is not a passive read; it is a 'roll up your sleeves, take a deep breath and dive in' experience. Leaving no stone unturned, Arata carefully guides his readers with a structured roadmap and journaling exercises that help the reader to clarify and finally realize his deepest wants and needs. Full of wisdom, *Wake Up, Man Up, Step Up* is a valuable tool on its own or as an adjunct to formal therapy."—**David N. Hafter, LMFT, author of** ***Growing Balls: Personal Power for Young Men***

"Ray's well-crafted, journal-style book could save men a lot of anguish and even lives. Far more than a crisis book, this step-by-step tool is a whole course in healthy adulthood. Begin now!"—**Bill Kauth, cofounder of the New Warrior Training Adventure of the ManKind Project and author of *A Circle of Men* and *We Need Each Other: Building Gift Community***

"The journey to authenticity is the most critical journey for all leaders of life. Ray Arata gives us the tools to step back in order to step up to our deepest, most sacred obligation: authentic, heartfelt service to all those we touch."—**Kevin Cashman, Senior Partner, CEO & Executive Development, Korn Ferry International, and author of *The Pause Principle: Step Back to Lead Forward* and *Leadership from the Inside Out***

"In *Wake Up, Man Up, Step Up: Transforming Your Wake-Up Call into Emotional Health and Happiness,* Ray Arata brings together his years of experience in the world of men's work and the world of business, to provide a clear, actionable, honest and easy-to-follow pathway to mature manhood. Having read many 'do-it-yourself' manhood books, Arata's offering is one that I will recommend to any man ready to take a pragmatic and heartfelt look at his life. *Wake Up, Man Up, Step Up* doesn't shy away from difficult cultural issues that men face, and it doesn't let men off the hook. If you're getting the 'wake-up' call in your life and are baffled about what to do next, buy this book. It's powerful, simple, and easy to follow. It *brings together the man who needs a clear plan and the man who is ready to slow down and look inside—and it gives them both a great set of steps to take.* As Arata points out, we can't do this work alone, and I'll be glad to have this book to share with men who are helping me on my journey."—**Boysen Hodgson, Communications & Marketing Director, the ManKind Project USA**

What Women Are Saying

"In *Wake Up, Man Up, Step Up,* Ray Arata masterfully demonstrates the masculine values he offers to guide decisions and behaviors for men to live happier, more fulfilled, purposeful lives. True to what he promises, this is a guidebook for a journey with plenty of options, choices and resources to have it be one's own journey. As a woman and an expert on gender differences, this book is a gift—a window into who everyday great men are and can be—from inside their world. His attention to the process is something I think women deeply appreciate and can connect to, from their world. There is something for women to know about themselves, as well, especially as one reflects on the essential influence of mother and father in our lives. Ray's 360-degree vision includes a 'Note to Women' to ground us in what is possible for ourselves and the men in our lives, and how we can best support the journey."—**Bonita Banducci, lecturer, *ENGENDERING GENDER COMPETENCE, Men and Women Building Effective Partnership in the Workplace* for a New Future for Business, Humanity and the Planet, School of Engineering Graduate Program, Santa Clara University**

"At last! This is the book women have been hoping for—the one to give to the men in their lives whom they adore; the one that will be received without any eye rolling! Ray Arata has written the ultimate man-to-man guidebook for men aching to fully wake up and live their truth. This book cuts right to the heart of what men need to hear and experience so they can live a life that fulfills them on all levels."—Amy Ahlers, The Wake-Up Call Coach and best-selling author of *Big Fat Lies Women Tell Themselves*

A Note from Emma Arata, Daughter

My dad asked me, "What kind of role model have I been for you as a man?"

That was an easy question, I thought. The answer was long and rolled off my tongue.

"You're not into that fake-macho BS. You know that being a man has nothing to do with how 'tough' you are. You take care of yourself and are emotionally aware. You aren't afraid to talk about feelings, or to ask for help. You have a strong voice and an equally strong presence and ability to listen. You understand the importance of communication. You hold yourself accountable and care about integrity and honesty. You are openly caring. You admit your weaknesses. You have morals and values that you can speak to. You are available and approachable. You can take charge and be a leader, but not for greed or desire to be powerful, and you listen to what others have to say."

My dad responded that he was so happy he could cry. He said that telling him he had modeled for me the attributes of a healthy, functioning, masculine man was the greatest gift I could give him.

But *I realized then that he was the one who had given me a greater gift than I could have ever asked for.* Because of my dad, I have a rock-solid picture in my head of what a real, good man should strive to be. I don't have to take seriously any of that "fake macho BS," and I have a checklist of things to look for in any man that I want to have in my life, which makes me stronger and more empowered.

WAKE UP,
MAN UP,
STEP UP

*Transforming Your Wake-Up Call
into Emotional Health
and Happiness*

Ray Arata

HIGHPOINT

www.highpointpubs.com

This edition published by Highpoint Life, an imprint of Highpoint Executive Publishing.

For information, write to info@highpointpubs.com.

First Edition

ISBN: 978-0-9839432-6-6

Library of Congress Cataloging-in-Publication Data

Arata, Ray

Wake Up, Man Up, Step Up

Summary: "*Wake Up, Man Up, Step Up* is an insightful and practical seven-step roadmap for how any man can transform large or small crises into opportunities for better relationships, happiness, and success."—Provided by publisher

ISBN: 978-0-9839432-6-6 (paperback)

1. Self-Help / Leadership

Library of Congress Control Number: 2012954895

Cover design by Joanne Shwed and Sarah Clarehart

Interior design and editing by Joanne Shwed

Manufactured in the United States of America

10 9 8 7 6 5 4 3 2 1

Contents

CHAPTER 3

Starting Your Journey 17

- *What is going on in your life that needs your attention?*

CHAPTER 4

- *How do you get backup?*

CHAPTER 5

- *What can you gain from speaking your truth to others?*

CHAPTER 8

- *What does your mother have to do with your present situation?*

CHAPTER 9

- *Why is it important to honor your parents?*

CHAPTER 12

- *How do you move forward responsibly?*

CHAPTER 13

- *How do you integrate this Roadmap process into other areas of your life?*

CHAPTER 14

- *What are the pillars of being the father your children need you to be?*

CHAPTER 15

- *What are the energies that make up a good partner and husband?*

Contents

CHAPTER 16

The Masculine Leader 167

- *What kind of leader in your personal and professional life do you aspire to be?*

Contents

CHAPTER 19

- *How can you encourage and support other men into being their "best man"?*

CHAPTER 20

CHAPTER 21

Acknowledgments

There are two women in my life who deserve unique credit for making this book a reality. The book would never have happened without both of their contributions. The first, by order of appearance, is my former wife and mother of our three wonderful children.

Margann, an uncharacteristic thank you for having the courage to call me on my stuff and seek a divorce, putting an end to my emotional illiteracy. My Men's Journey started because of you. Thanks for being a great mom and demanding the best from me as a father ... still.

The biggest heartfelt thank you goes out to my wife and best friend Anna. You were a big part of my inspiration to keep working on myself over the years. Thank you for your encouragement to write this book and your patience, despite my myopic focus, which had me occasionally forget that there are more important things in life than my book, namely you, the kids, and my career. Thanks for allowing me the space to dream.

I wish to acknowledge my daughter Emma for her courage to go inward, to challenge me, and to be a reminder for me of the huge responsibility I have as her father and its direct influence on her as the first "real man" in her life.

Thank you Evan Lurie for introducing me to my book coach, Joel Orr. I needed a coach and what I got was a lot more.

Joel, thanks for being a friend, a mentor, a wise sage, a great coach, and a remarkably warm father-like figure when I needed it. We both know I need that a lot during those times I struggled. Thanks from the bottom of my heart.

A refreshing and cheerful thank you to Taylor Ray, my first editor, who amazed me and challenged me time and time again with her curiosity, femininity, vulnerability, and boundless energy. You captured my voice as if it were your own. Thanks for holding nothing back.

As I am not one for attending to details, my copyeditor, Joanne Shwed, deserves a big thank you for dragging me through the muck with a great attitude, listening to my rants and raves, and doing the real dirty work of making the book flow and tie together. It was such a relief to experience the ease and grace Joanne provided in choosing the best layout for my book. Writing a book followed by editing a book is hard work; when it comes to the layout and cover design, it all becomes real ... and fun!

I also want to acknowledge my new friend Joe Stauffacher who, in addition to helping me with my Internet marketing, also chipped in his neuro-linguistic programming training and edited the book as well.

There are and have been several influential men in my life for whom I drew inspiration to write this book. First, my father, whose name I claim, who fathered me well, and who modeled numerous aspects of what it means to be a man.

Second, my sons Aidan and Enzo, the next generation of young men. They are going to need every man whom I can inspire to go on their men's journey and be part of their world as they grow into fine, young, responsible men, able to step fully into their roles as husbands, fathers, leaders, and friends.

Third, my best friend John Emerson, who taught me what real male friendships are all about.

Last, but certainly not least, is God. I made the decision and commitment to write the book and had no clue as to how long it would take or where I would find the time. The saying, "God works in mysterious ways," couldn't be truer. I was running on a path, didn't see the little rock, tripped on it, broke my foot, and rendered me unable to do anything for 10 weeks except write this book. Thank you God for that little rock.

Preface: A Man Who Has Lived and Learned

When I decided to write this book, it was largely at the prompting of individuals close to me as well as many men whom I had helped get through personal crises related to their behavior, relationships with women, and sense of identity. Basically, I wrote this to share my knowledge and experience for the benefit of other men.

I wanted to make the journey of male introspection doable for those who were ready because it appeared that attending an introductory weekend or even joining a group was perhaps an unrealistically big jump for many men.

A book—or, better yet, a *guidebook*—that meets men where they are and lays out a path to self-awareness, understanding, and happiness … now that's a different story! Who better to write the book than someone who has gone on the path?

My belief then and now is that *if I can do this, so can you.*

This is not a therapy book although, according to my friend David Hafter, MFT, it is a valuable tool on its own or as an adjunct to formal therapy. I am a self-educated man who continually seeks new knowledge from others. Since I am not a psychologist, therapist, counselor, or "self-described guru," I wrote in a manner consistent with how I am in the world: a man who has done extensive personal work and is committed to supporting other men on their journey of emotional maturity.

I want to share what's behind the prescriptive feel of the book so you may appreciate my background and qualifications for writing it.

Here are my life experiences that led to the material in the book:

- A conscious divorce (now in its 12th year) with the mother of my three children

- My second marriage (now in its 10th year) to my life partner Anna

- My nuclear family's battle with addiction and my role in their intervention(s)

- My daughter's battle with and her successful recovery from an eating disorder

- My two sons' initiation into manhood

- An intimate relationship with my best male friend John and all it taught me

- My challenging career transition (now in its sixth year)

My adaption, role, and surrender to all of these experiences would not have been possible without the following:

- Individual, couples, and family therapy

- My facilitation, teaching, and leadership development on 50+ men's training workshops, including money workshops, life planning trainings, and Folsom Prison training

- My leadership training within the context of my leader path in the Mankind Project and independent trainings

- Approximately 3,000 hours in men's trainings, 2,000 hours of men's groups, 2,000 hours of individual coaching, and 1,500 hours of leadership coaching

- Mondo Zen meditation training ("Hollow Bones")

These people and their work have indirectly influenced me:

- Debbie Ford (shadow work)
- Joseph Campbell (Hero's Journey)
- John Wellwood (relationships)
- Alison Armstrong (relationships)
- Kevin Cashman (leadership)
- Miguel Ruiz (The Four Agreements)
- Junpo Dennis Kelly (meditation)

The tendency for most guys is to go it alone, which is our Achilles Heel. Your intuition, your heart, your mind, and your soul all are available to successfully navigate your wake-up call.

My hope in sharing what is behind my writings—namely, my life experiences—is that you can begin to trust me and eventually yourself.

There is no need to do this alone. *Let's go!*

Prologue

It took seven months to complete our brand new, custom-built home, and my family—my wife of seven years and our three children—lived next door while it was being built. I was in the new house barely two months before the storm blew in. At the time, I was hitting my stride as a retirement planning consultant in the financial industry. I was making great money, living in California's Marin County, and everything seemed fine.

Then, I walked into the office one day and learned that one of my partners had left our firm to join another. This guy was my friend, and I heard the news from a colleague without a warning or heads up. It felt like a punch in the gut. I felt fear surrounding my ability to maintain my lifestyle, especially since I had finished renovating my house and increased my mortgage.

Two weeks later, 1:00 a.m. and pitch black outside, I was lying in bed, awake. I heard my wife breathing. She was also awake but silent—the loud kind of silence, the heavy kind of silence. Something was keeping her up.

By all outward appearances, everything should have been great. Our house was done, our three children were asleep in their own wing of the house, the stock market was climbing, and my income was rising … but I couldn't sleep.

My dad always told me never to ask a question unless you were ready for the answer, so I considered my next words carefully.

"Is something bothering you, honey?"

Her answer was not what I was expecting. Something wasn't bothering her; plenty of things were bothering her—namely me, our marriage, and the fact that our life (and my life, specifically) was about to change. She said she was discontented with our marriage and didn't love me anymore. She told me she had tried numerous times to get my attention and just couldn't handle it any longer.

I was clueless. I felt as if someone had dropped a Volkswagen on my head.

My wake-up call as a man occurred in May 1999. Whether or not I liked it, the process of waking up was a challenging one.

Ten months later, I moved out; two months after that, we were in the process of going through a divorce, and my life and the lives of our children were changed forever.

The process of "waking up" has been my journey and inspiration. In this book, which is written for you, I will show you how to answer your wake-up call and offer suggestions about what you can make of your life as you strive to be a better man in your roles as husband, father, leader, businessman, and friend.

Maybe a Volkswagen hasn't dropped on your head yet, but maybe you're starting to feel the impending weight. Maybe you've already experienced the shock of change. Regardless of where you are in your life, I invite you to dive into this book and consider your journey in becoming the man you want to be.

CHAPTER 1

The Wake-Up Call

Why did this happen and what is the opportunity?

What is a Wake-Up Call?

A "wake-up call" is a shock, a surprise, or a realization that causes you to become fully alert to what is happening in your life. If you have ever experienced a wake-up call, you probably did not choose what it would be like. I also refer to a wake-up call as a glimpse into a moment of truth, where you can see that staying on your current trajectory and not changing only means more pain.

Do Any of These Situations Sound Familiar?

- Your relationship is on the rocks and you want to save it.
- You are in the divorce process and you don't want to go down with the ship.
- You are having difficulty fathering; your teenagers may be challenging you.

- Your life lacks purpose and passion; you are tired and feel burned out.

- You are having difficulty leading in your business or work life.

- You have a career of many years, but it's killing you to keep doing it.

- Many financial aspects of your life seem tough and never ending.

- You (or a close friend) survived a health or death scare, which scared the crap out of you, and now you are re-evaluating *everything*!

- You struggle with what it means to be a man in your various life roles.

- You are lonely and in need of some *real* male friends whom you can count on.

- You are in recovery and want to continue your growth.

- Nothing is as it used to be; you're in midlife with lots of questions but not a lot of answers.

- None of the above applies *exactly*, but things still aren't right in your life.

Most men in the above situations have no clue what to do. If you're like most guys in crisis, you simply want to know what to do next because, if you knew what to do, *you would already be doing it!*

Like many men, you are not sure whether to interpret this type of situation at face value or as something much deeper and more profound. Is this crisis trying to tell you something? Again, if you knew the answer to this question, things would seem more manageable and you wouldn't feel so shaken up.

Interpreting Your Call

I encourage you to check in with your own pain tolerance of the crisis at hand, and consider that your wake-up call is simply an external symptom of something deep inside you that is longing for a shift. This wake-up call has occurred because *the man you want to be* and *the man you are meant to be* are now called forth to show up in all your masculinity and maturity. This man is demanding to come out and show up.

If you take the point of view that your wake-up call is an awakening—asking you to becoming fully alert to your life *as it is* so you can consciously move forward and be the man you want to be—you will have taken the first step towards a more full and potent life.

If you embrace this point of view, you can make just about anything happen.

Being in "The Tunnel"

If you have experienced a wake-up call, chances are that you are somewhere between your mid-thirties to late fifties (with exceptions, of course). You may also be experiencing emotional discomfort in the form of anger, anxiety, fear, confusion, and even apathy. You may even be bored.

What once was clear to you may no longer be obvious. The tried-and-true fixes that used to work may not work anymore, and you're not sure what side is up. Things that used to hold your attention and excite you no longer do. To top it off, few of your male friends—and the woman or partner in your life—possess the depth to support you in a healthy way. Life just isn't right—or at least it isn't what it *used* to be.

These feelings result from being in "The Tunnel" (Alison Armstrong, *Keys to the Kingdom*, PAX Programs Incorporated, 2003). Many people refer to this collection of confusing symptoms as a "midlife crisis," but I assert that this situation is quite the opposite. Nothing is broken here; in fact, you are "in between" stages in a very important transition of your life as a man.

Consider your wake-up call and experience in The Tunnel as your midlife *opportunity,* and what you choose to do with this opportunity is up to you. I invite you to see this experience as an opportunity for you to answer the call that has been inside of you and all men: *Be the man you want to be in your life roles as a man.* If you do this, many of the successes you seek will follow.

The people in your life (and everyone else on the planet) need you to answer this call in a way that serves others and yourself. The intent of this book is to assist you on your path to moving through The Tunnel and coming out the other side as the man you want to be in your life.

Ignoring the Call

Of course, all of this is your choice. You could ignore the signs of your wake-up call and keep living your life exactly as you have been living it. You could shake off the health or death scare of a friend or loved one, and forget how it made you feel about life. You could ignore the implications of a divorce, blame everyone else, remarry, and do it all over again. You could quit your job, do drugs, drink yourself to death, or just plain give up.

However, since you bought or were given this book and have read it this far, I can say the following with confidence: *You could resist, but that's not why you're here.*

Saddling Up

I've mentioned this already, but I want to be very clear: If you're willing to do it, answering your wake-up call starts with making a commitment—right now—to embark on a journey … Your Men's Journey (yourmensjourney.com).

As a precursor to experiencing this journey in the best possible light, I ask that you consider making seven specific agreements with yourself—referred to as Seven Growth Stretches—that will lay the foundation for what you are willing to do as you turn and face your wake-up call.

A "stretch" is a promise to do something new for your personal growth, usually encompassing more supportive behaviors. It is a first "new step" that is attainable and challenging at the same time. The solidness of your commitment to these growth stretches is vital because it directly affects the success of Your Men's Journey towards change.

Seven Growth Stretches

1. **Be willing to look at yourself.** This agreement starts with acknowledging your present situation and all its foibles, being curious about how these events came to be and how you were involved, and blaming no one else for where you are.

2. **Be willing to learn about yourself.** Once you have committed to looking at yourself, there is a lot to learn. This includes discovering what has driven your behaviors and in what ways these influences have played out, and learning about the repressed self-beliefs and behaviors, which relate to these beliefs, wreaking havoc in your relationships and in your life.

3. **Be willing to learn from other men.** For thousands of years, men have initiated other men into their masculine birthright; today is no different. For you, these men can be peers, coaches, uncles, sons, grandfathers, fathers, therapists, and elders in your community. It is important to recognize that men are stronger together than separately, and your male support network (even if you don't have one yet) is source of wisdom and stability.

4. **Be willing to learn about those who influenced you.** When you were young, you were impressionable. You were vulnerable to shaping by parental figures, and the events in your early life had a powerful emotional effect on you. As a kid, you watched your parent(s), and what they believed and did influenced your own beliefs and behaviors in positive and negative ways. Being willing to learn about these influential people is an important element of being able to act more consciously as you move forward.

5. **Be open and willing to act on new choices.** Once you have looked at yourself and learned who and what influenced you, recognize that you possess the ability to make new choices and act on them. New choices will produce different and more desirable results in important areas of your life.

6. **Be willing to take responsibility for your actions in the past and in the future.** Being the man you are meant to be requires accountability, which is defined as taking full responsibility for your words, choices, and actions as well as their consequences—intended or not. For men, being able to be accountable is the cornerstone of personal integrity.

7. **Be willing to apply what you learn to your everyday life.** As you go through the exercises in this book, you will be ready to choose the relevant areas in your life in which to apply your new knowledge. Apply what you learn to the area of your life most important to you now. Then, when you are done with one area of your life, you will have the tools to work on other areas.

These Seven Growth Stretches are designed to help you look at yourself, forgive yourself (and others), and be able to make new choices that will ensure more positive results in your life. They commit you to a learning path; however, in all fairness, I need to let you know that the road ahead may get rocky at times.

I believe the saying, "Something really good is often worth fighting for." You may find parts of this journey very challenging. Even if you've never done anything like this before, remember that there is a light at the end of the tunnel if you do the work.

It's a lot like riding a bike; in other words, how you intend to *be* as a man correlates directly to that joy you may have felt as a young boy while on a bike (or a horse or a skateboard). The courage you had to "get back on" the bike after you fell off when you were learning to ride is the same courage I will ask you to tap into while you are on Your Men's Journey.

I divided the book into several sections so you can navigate your own process at a pace that feels right to you. Being on Your Men's Journey will also require some personal awareness skills, which I will help you build through the action steps and exercises that accompany many of the chapters.

Use this book as your map. Ultimately, my intention is for you to become your own guide, use the tools in this book whenever you need them, and become aligned with the powerful, respectable, better man that lives inside you.

CHAPTER 2

What to Do First

How do you transition from crisis?

Starting Your Men's Journey

It is important to recognize where you are in the wake-up call process and then decide what to do first.

Do any of the following scenarios describe your situation?

- The Volkswagen may have just dropped on your head.

- The dust may have settled and you're wondering what to do next.

- You may have read several self-help books and had some therapy, and you're questioning how it all fits together.

- This may be the first time in your life when you've been asked to face yourself.

- You have successfully gone through a recovery program and now realize that your next area to confront is the underlying pain, which you were trying to numb.

Wherever you are, and whatever is happening in your life, you need to do several things before you start Your Men's Journey. These ideas may seem simple (or obvious) at first, and they are worth some real exploration if you are going to be fully prepared for what is ahead.

- **Face the fact that you have feelings.** They are yours to experience and own. This is not some wimpy, fluffy statement; it is a hard-hitting truth. Feelings are signals that keep you alive and on your own path. Ignoring your feelings leads to trouble (and louder wake-up calls); getting to know your feelings and owning them are essential to achieving success in Your Men's Journey.

- **Stabilize crisis situations.** The personal work you'll need to do to make significant changes in your life (and become the man you want to be) is twice as difficult to complete when more urgent life concerns are weighing you down.

- **Commit to following a structured process (or roadmap).** This book is a culmination of hundreds of conversations, workshops, articles, and experiences dealing with men in crisis who want to make something better of their lives. If you want to make a major shift, you've got to go full out. Following a structure, such as the seven-step Roadmaps in this book, will allow you to build on what you learn. It will also give you enough forward momentum so you can see where you're heading and where you've been.

- **Buy a journal and commit to writing in it.** I invite you to invest the money and the time into buying and using a journal. This book has a lot of reflective and introspective questions and exercises that require journal entries (221 to be exact!). Resist the reaction of being overwhelmed. These questions are here to help you. You may want to read through them first without putting pen to paper. When you are ready, you can decide when you want to take the deep dive, as this will be one of many acts of faith that will pay off big time. Feel free to write short answers—whatever works for you. In certain instances, I pose questions to simply ponder and expand your awareness; for others, I ask that you write down answers so, in subsequent areas of the book when I reference prior answers, your answers will serve you twice. Whether you choose to answer them is your choice, and so is the degree to which you answer them. Consider these questions as an opportunity to open your mind and "glimpse into you." You will get out of it what you put into it. When problems come back up for you, you can go to one section or another from your journal to get reminders of your priorities, values, and plans.

Acknowledge Feelings (Like a Man)

Men are not known for having a rich vocabulary of feelings; in fact, feeling anything other than "all right" or "good" is often considered stupid or girlish. Few men receive any kind of male modeling in expressing the full range of feelings. When I ask men if there is a proper role in their life for their feelings, I usually get a predictable set of answers: "What are they? How do I feel them? What exactly is the point?"

The old "tough-guy model" of not showing feelings (modeled by many fathers) meant that the only option for feelings was to bury them. This behavior has been going on for generations. The result? Many men—including you—pay the price in the form of feeling isolated, being in strained relationships, feeling stuck, hurting others, and being hurt.

Without any training for how to process or express what's going on inside, many men act out rage and toxic anger and feel shame—all of which is often put on the ones closest to them and to the ones they love the most.

If I were to hazard a guess, I'd say that being out of touch with your own feelings is one of the factors that led to your current wake-up call.

Know this: *Ignoring your feelings means ignoring your life.*

From one man to another, I am going to ask you to reconsider your view of feelings: how you view them, express them, understand them, and even invite them. It's natural to want to express what you're feeling; however, as a man, you probably don't know how to do this because you haven't been shown and were never given permission.

More importantly, *your feelings are an additional source of your truth as a man.* Feelings exist in your body, and your body knows what you feel before your minds does.

Core Feelings

Am I asking you to become suddenly fluent in a new language? No. I'm just asking you to recognize several core feelings, and to start paying attention if you feel any of them at any given moment:

- **Sadness/grief:** You had something very important and now it's gone.

- **Anger:** You can't get what you want. Something is blocking it. Something is in the way.

- **Joy:** You have what you want and you're happy.

- **Fear:** Something is coming and it's dangerous. It is going to wipe you out.

- **Shame:** You have a negative self-judgment and think that you are bad.

Note that "guilt" is a feeling of sadness or fear for something you did (you *did* something bad) versus "shame," which is sadness or fear about yourself (you *are* bad).

Answer the following questions and write them in your journal:

✍️ JOURNAL ENTRY #1

Take a deep breath. Which of the core feelings listed above is closest to what you are feeling right now? Disappointment (sadness/grief)? Excitement (joy)? Nervousness or anxiety (fear)? If you can't pick a core feeling, focus on any sensations in your body. Is your chest tight? Does your stomach ache? Be as descriptive as possible about what you are experiencing.

Transition from Crisis Mode

If you are experiencing a crisis situation in your life right now, you will need to attend to it before you start Your Men's Journey. The work of this process will take some time and attention, and you'll want to have space in your life to deal with things fully.

Transitioning from crisis mode is possible, but first take a frank look at your life and assess what is happening in it. Look for areas that may need your *complete attention* right now. These areas may be vitally important, and what is happening could be damaging to your physical health, emotional health, relationships, or financial well-being. Consider the following as you evaluate what you might need to do.

Assess the Areas in Your Life Where You May Be In Crisis

- Are you financially unstable and spending more than you make?

- Does your health need your attention right now?

- Are your children in trouble and need you to intervene?

- Are you in an unhealthy co-dependent relationship that is dangerous to your emotional health?

- Is your work-life equation seriously out of balance?

- Have you lost or are you about to lose your job?

- Is any part of your life out of control?

Recognize and Admit That You Are in Crisis

This is the first step towards being able to do something about it. Can you face your present reality and see things as they are, or are you in denial? By confronting your crisis state, it actually allows you to do something about it.

Prioritize

Figure out which situation(s) are most urgent. I recommend that you focus your priorities on your physical and emotional health followed by your financial health. Everything else can follow. If you are unhealthy physically or emotionally, it makes it difficult for you to be effective in other areas.

Stabilize

If you were to do nothing about this situation, would it get better by itself or get worse? This is a trick question because you already know the answer. The reality is that this is probably what you have been *hoping for,* but hoping for a change hasn't worked. See if you can acknowledge any truth here.

What do you need to do to stabilize your crisis so you can function on a daily basis and avoid creating more chaos for yourself or for others? If situations in your life, such as a health or financial emergency, are threatening your ability to function daily and require your immediate attention, I recommend that you put this book down and *focus your attention on stabilizing your situation.*

If your situation is less dire, consider the following situational remedies:

- You might need to put together a budget where your spending and earning are in alignment, and you might need professional assistance to do this.

- You might need to see a doctor or therapist—or both.

- You might need to intervene with your teenagers.

- You might need to leave your relationship and live in separate, neutral places.

- You might need to ask for help at work to improve your performance so you don't lose your job.

- You might need to go into a 30-day treatment facility for your addiction(s). If you are going to take Your Men's Journey seriously, you need to be sober and have your mental faculties available to you (without any kind of drugs in your system that are messing with your head). In order to have a successful experience of navigating your wake-up call, it is important that you are in a stable place with the physical, mental, and emotional areas of your life.

This is a great opportunity to seek the counsel of a professional therapist. Whether you are using a substance or suffer from porn/sex addiction, working with a therapist on self-forgiveness before you go on Your Men's Journey would be wise.

Many men are in the same situation. If you don't like to ask for help, that's OK; most men don't. As you will see, asking for help and getting the help you need are powerful acts. These acts will show that you are serious about being a better man and being able to act on this commitment. These acts are demonstrations of your vulnerability—a true sign of strength.

Follow a Roadmap

Having a map on a trip is always a good idea because it makes the journey much easier when you know that someone has gone before you to point out the routes, options, hazards, and special points of interest. At a minimum, you know that someone has already explored the territory, and it can relieve your stress in trying to figure out the best way to get where you're headed. All you need to do is focus on "going."

I have created a seven-step Roadmap to guide you on Your Men's Journey—a deliberately ordered structure on which you may rely to get you where you want to go.

Having supported and coached many men, the order of these Roadmap steps came from my clients' experiences and the many men I supported along the way, taking into account how men are typically wired. For this reason, it's important to adhere to the Roadmap steps sequentially because they include activities that are part of a much larger process. If you skip steps, you will miss the important building blocks that create a foundation for the changes you need to make.

CHAPTER 3

Starting Your Journey

What is going on in your life that needs your attention?

Take a Closer Look

When you're heading out on a rigorous trip, you need to pack your stuff (and you may want to get in shape). I designed this chapter to help you think about several things that will make Your Men's Journey focused and powerful.

Many people (including men) try to avoid looking at the impact of their actions on their life and relationships because these results are difficult to confront, acknowledge, and possibly forgive. Many men feel powerless to change things, so it seems easier to look the other way, numb out, or blame someone else without any particular ownership. This pattern usually ensures a wake-up call of some sort; often, the stronger the resistance to addressing what's actually happening, the louder the wake-up call.

The good news is that opposite forces are also at work. The stronger your willingness to turn your attention and intention towards the area in life that needs your attention, *the more power you have to change it.* This means that there is actually power in putting your attention towards something … even if it's the not-so-good stuff.

Taking a closer look at yourself includes evaluating the realities of your romantic relationships, male friendships, parenting role, career, purpose, leadership, finances, and health *as they are.* It means acknowledging the consequences to yourself and to others in the midst of acknowledging how you show up in these relationships. Are your relationships where you want them to be? Is there trust, truth, and intimacy or are there distrust, stories that you make up about the truth, and disconnection?

Some men can't handle taking on this task. They look the other way and continue as they have before, and the wake-up call will only ring more loudly for them. The simple option, in masculine terms, is to *face the truth as it presently is.*

If you truly wish to step up and take Your Men's Journey to be a more mature and evolved man in the important areas of your life, choose and make the hard decisions. Before you can change anything about your life, you must confront the results of how you have been living your life. This confrontation takes courage.

You don't have to change anything right now; you just have to look at it and "be with it." This action takes forgiveness of yourself and of other people, and it takes guts. *Do you have guts?*

See What Is: Confronting Hard Truths

In this section, I will ask you some pointed questions about yourself. I invite you to consider this exercise as an opportunity to be honest with yourself. While this may be uncomfortable, your honesty will give you a better chance to frame a new set of outcomes for your life in a positive way.

The following seven themes—Seven Reality Checkpoints—may help you take a closer and more honest look at how you are showing up with the people in your life right now. Read each of the sections, ponder the questions, evaluate what is true, and notice any resistance or feelings that may arise. Your answers to these questions will support you in taking a deeper look into specific and relevant areas in your life in the subsequent section.

Pay special attention to the areas that seem to provoke some kind of reaction (like defensiveness or blame) and come back to those areas later to see if you can answer the questions more humbly. Remember that *these questions are only for you.* Sharing them with others is optional. The more honest you are with yourself the better.

Seven Reality Checkpoints

1. **Presence and focus.** Be with your family when you are in their company and focus your attention on them.

   Example of this assessment before my wake-up call: I often worked away from home and, when I was there, I was often on the phone. My wife used to say, "When you are here, you're not … put your feet on the ground and be here!"

   - When you are with your wife, partner, friends, or kids, do you only focus on them? Do you often feel as if there's too much to do and too much to think about?

   - How much of your attention do you give to others?

   - How alone or disconnected do you feel when you are with others?

- Are you inside you own head or present with your surroundings?

2. **Ability to listen to understand.** Demonstrate interest and curiosity about other people and about what they are saying. Waiting for the other person to finish so you can talk is the wrong idea of being present.

Example of this assessment before my wake-up call: Having the ability to "listen to understand" my wife or myself was a foreign concept. As a result, I missed several clues and insights about her. I asked "What's your point?" or "What's the problem?" and then tried to fix it. I also made it about me and tried to defend it. This contributed to her emotional departure.

- Do you listen without going into solution mode or are you trying to fix others' problems?

- Are you already forming what you want to say while other people are still talking?

- Do you have a genuine curiosity in learning what people are saying?

- Do other people confide in you?

3. **Attention to others' needs.** Pay attention to the needs (that you can provide) of those who are in a relationship with you while maintaining your needs, and find the balance between the two. Listen to hints, write stuff down, and follow through. This requires you to actually be curious about and interested in others' needs.

Example of this assessment before my wake-up call: I was inattentive to my wife's needs and more focused on what wasn't happening *for me,* and I pouted when she didn't figure me out. I didn't pay attention to learning about her and what was important *to her.* I never knew what to buy for her birthday or for Christmas because I missed her clues. This was largely due to my inability to be there for myself; in other words, if I couldn't do it for myself, then how could I do it for anyone else?

- Do you demonstrate an interest in what's important to your loved ones?

- Do you make an effort to care for them?

4. **Responsibility for my needs.** Do you take full responsibility for giving yourself what you need?

Example of this assessment before my wake-up call: I was inattentive to my needs and often asked my wife for permission or made her responsible for my needs without communicating them clearly. I ended up creating a guessing game for my wife to play, which often created a let down for both of us because she didn't know what I wanted. This meant that Christmas and birthdays revisited my past because my mother never understood me. In addition, when my wife did get me something to demonstrate that she understood me, I didn't know how to handle it because "being seen and known" was a foreign feeling. I realize now that, back then, I didn't "get" myself. I have learned that knowing me—and giving myself what I need—are *my responsibilities.*

- Can you recognize your needs and give them to yourself?

- Are you clear about your own needs and do you take responsibility for meeting them, or do you put that on someone else?

- When you need help, do you ask for it?

5. **Anger management.** Anger is a big issue for many men. In this section, I invite you to ask yourself several questions simply to see what shows up. Later in the book, I will facilitate you towards helpful solutions; for now, just notice your answers.

    Do you react uncontrollably towards others when you are angry?

    Example of this assessment before my wake-up call: In my first marriage, I would often get angry for a variety of reasons, and show up in a less-than-stellar fashion. I would typically yell and raise my voice when I was angry. As a result, when this happened, my wife didn't feel safe and she would go away.

    - When you get upset, do you contain your anger or put it on others?

    - Are you aware of how your anger affects others?

    - Do you have regular outlets for your anger?

    - What is true about your anger? Are you typically sad, afraid, or grieving a loss?

    - Has your anger cost you some relationships in your life?

6. **Emotional literacy.** Are you conscious of your feelings? Are you aware of your behaviors associated with those feelings? Are you aware of how those feelings affect others so you can change your behavior as you learn more about yourself?

    Example of this assessment before my wake-up call: I was not in touch with my feelings and my emotional literacy was more on the illiterate side. I was not in touch with my sadness, fear, or shame—all of which typically manifested through anger. When and if I were upset, I tried to hide it. There was little congruence to what I was feeling on the inside and how it showed on the outside. The result? I lost my wife's trust in me, which created more separation.

- Are you in touch with your feelings? Do you know what the core feelings are (e.g., sadness/grief, anger, joy, fear, and shame)?

- Do you know how to talk about your feelings?

- Do you regularly experience sadness or other "negative" emotions?

- Do others say they can trust you?

7. **Integrity.** Do your words and actions match your ethics, such as adherence to moral and ethical principles, the soundness of your moral character, and honesty?

Example of this assessment before my wake-up call: I repeatedly abused my integrity because I was choosing different actions from what I was saying. Eventually, my wife stopped trusting me and my apologies soon carried no weight.

- Do you do what you say you are going to do?

- Do you remember what you say you are going to do?

- How well do you pay attention when you make commitments?

- How quickly do you let others know when you can't make your commitments?

- When others break their agreements with you, do you let them slide or do you speak up?

Other Areas of Your Life to Examine Using the Seven Reality Checkpoints

In addition to the quality of your relationships, you may want to look at other important areas in your life. The questions that follow each section are for you to ponder at this point in Your Men's Journey.

As an example, I offer my abbreviated and reflective perspective to give you an idea of the things for which one father (me) strived after his wake-up call. The following example is nothing more than a glimpse of what could be possible for you.

As I began my journey of being a better man, my focus (as a father of three) had to be on the emotional, physical, mental, and spiritual health of my kids. When my divorce changed things significantly, my awareness of all areas of parenting—and the very real responsibility of what this meant—translated to one thing: *I realized that I needed to attend to my own emotional, physical, mental, and spiritual health because I was the model upon which they would seek to emulate.*

I needed to do my own work so I could "show up" as a present father. My actions are my children's teacher, and my children are my teacher. Some of the hard lessons I learned about "showing up" very much applied to my fathering.

Because my divorce limited my time with my kids by at least half, I had to make the most of my time with them. Dinner table time, breakfast rituals, homework time, and a goodnight ritual gave us something to look forward to. The consistency of these rituals exists to this day as my teenagers still sit on my bed to say goodnight.

When my kids were little, I often struggled with activities and then realized that it didn't matter as long as I was with them; unfortunately, I would try to multitask. It used to bug my kids (and my wife) when I was always on the phone when I was with them. I realized that all they wanted was *my attention,* which was what I wanted when I was young. I still wonder how much attention my paternal grandfather gave my father.

Because I had a strong mother, who did most of the day-to-day disciplining, I often deferred to the mother of my children to administer the discipline, which left me to be the "softie." This caused problems and, to this day, I continue to consciously improve on my behavior. I have had to unwind this dynamic over the years and relieve the mother of my children of this sole responsibility. It gives her more room to be a "soft mommy." It unifies our parenting, despite the fact that we live in different homes.

My personal work has mainly been around my anger and the management of my energy. My unregulated and unhealed anger would surface as yelling. I yelled a lot and this hurt my kids emotionally.

Over time, I realized the gigantic responsibility and high stakes in dealing with my emotions. I had to forgive myself for wounding my kids in the past. This realization motivated me to begin My Men's Journey; if I didn't, I would repeatedly inflict my emotional baggage onto my kids.

I now view my children as my teachers and messengers of how I show up in the world. Whenever they are being themselves and provoke a reaction in me, I remember that they have given me an opportunity to look at and learn about myself. I can then share with them my results and be a better parent for it. They usually (I say *usually*) appreciate it.

The following questions are entirely subjective and can be answered from many perspectives—and they are all correct. I suggest you spend some time thinking about these questions and ponder them honestly. What matters are *your* answers.

Fatherhood

- Are you being the best father you can be?
- How would you describe quality time with your kids?
- How well do you discipline? Do you discipline?

Spouse/Partner

- Do you attend to your significant other's needs to the detriment of yourself?
- Is your anger management an issue in your relationship?
- Are you out of integrity with your significant other?

Money

- Is your financial house in order?
- Do you argue with your spouse about money or do you avoid talking about it altogether?
- Do any areas around money, such as spending, saving, managing, or investing, make you feel uncomfortable?
- Do any areas of your financial realm need your attention?

Leadership

- Are you leading in your life and in your business?
- Do you have the respect and allegiance of your employees and/or co-workers?

- Do you lead in your family?

- Do you shy away from leadership?

Male Friendships

- Do you have quality supportive male friendships?

- Are there quality men in your life with whom you spend time?

- Do you get support from these quality men?

- Are there men in your life whom you trust?

- Do these guys challenge you and hold you accountable?

- Do these guys support your growth?

Health

- Do you eat regularly (i.e., not go long periods without food)?

- Are there things you know you "should" do for your health and choose to avoid?

- Do you have a health problem you know of and should get advice for and choose to avoid?

- Do you exercise regularly?

- How stressed out are you on a regular basis?

- Do you sleep well?

- Do you enjoy other activities besides work? Do you do them every week?

If you're slightly overwhelmed by these questions, that's OK. Take a deep breath. Maybe the way you go through life doesn't ask you to stop and consider your life this deeply. Taking a hard look at your life is essential if you want to improve it, so feel free to review these questions often or as many times as necessary.

Masculine Core Values

Throughout Your Men's Journey, you will need to rely on an internal compass. This compass will keep you oriented in the right direction and signal you if you get off track. This compass won't be something you hold in your hand; it will be something *inside you* that will always be there when you choose to use it.

Your internal compass contains your values, and values guide you when you connect to them. An influential male figure in your life could have handed down your masculine core values, derived and ingrained from your experiences. These masculine core values (or the absence of them) influence your experience as a man and your behavior.

Values feel "natural" and "right" on gut and heart levels. They are the filter upon which you live and make decisions. Your values form the basis of how you approach your life, and your values drive your behaviors. When you consciously set your priorities in accordance with your stated values, you experience less stress and pressure and more confidence, ease, and inner strength.

Values provide people with strength and a sense of purpose, which means that a man with a strong sense of his core values is a man with masculine certainty. Standing up for who you are and actively living your values are examples of your strength as a man.

Here is an exercise to get at or come up with your masculine core values to serve you on Your Men's Journey. These values may—and often will—support your other values.

These masculine core values are common to many men:

- **Vitality:** Having energy, and being strong and active

- **Authenticity:** Being true to your personality, spirit, or character, and speaking to that truth

- **Honor:** Being honest and fair, and doing the right thing, which includes being honest with yourself and others

- **Integrity:** Displaying in word and deed that you are committed to the values, beliefs, and principles you claim to hold

- **Accountability:** Taking full responsibility for your words, actions and choices, and their consequences—intended or not

Other values exist, of course. These are the major masculine core values that resonate with many men whom I have encountered over the years—both personally and professionally. My nonadherence to these masculine core values is what caused my pain in my former marriage, and my conscious adherence to these values continues to influence my decisions and behaviors to this day.

The following exercise will help you either adapt or create two or more masculine core values that work for you. You will be referring to these values in Chapter 6, "Roadmap Step #3—Declare Your Want," and Chapter 12, "Roadmap Step # 6—Embody Responsibility," when reflecting on questions and forming your personal growth plan(s).

Discovering Your Masculine Core Values Exercise

Take the time, eliminate any distractions, and write down the answers to the following questions in your journal:

✍ JOURNAL ENTRY #2

Think about a relationship with your father, grandfather, uncle, older brother, or coach, and ask yourself if there are two or three milestone or life-changing events that affected you where this person acted like a man (or not). Write down all the positive or negative events.

✍ JOURNAL ENTRY #3

If these events were positive, write down the values that made it so satisfying; if they were negative, write down the values that were absent or threatening that made it so unsatisfying.

Go through this process on your own initially, and then consider talking to someone about each event to help you achieve greater clarity.

✍ JOURNAL ENTRY #4

Looking across all of the events, choose two or three values that matter the most to you.

✍ JOURNAL ENTRY #5

Take the time to define what these values mean to you.

Your masculine core values may differ from other men. When you define your values, you have something concrete, and you may want to check in when making decisions and setting priorities. Whether your goal is to be a better leader, spouse, parent, businessman, or friend, these masculine core values will help you achieve that ultimate "win."

Don't take my word for it … see for yourself!

The Light at the End of the Tunnel

If you've looked at your life a little more closely, and have identified your masculine core values, imagine what might happen if you actively answer your wake-up call! What positive things might you experience? *What is it* that would make Your Men's Journey worth it? What is your light at the end of the tunnel? Who do you want to be as a man and in what capacity?

Answering these questions will give you the opportunity to script the light at the end of your tunnel. It will give you control around the things that matter most in your life, because the light is *your t*arget—and *your* reason—to go on Your Men's Journey and to maintain the course to seek that light.

Take a moment to put aside any anxiety, confusion, or jumbled emotions, and give yourself the opportunity to be open to the possibilities presented to you. Imagine writing "I will" statements about things you value—things you want to be or have by the time Your Men's Journey is complete. How do you want to reflect on your life? What is your legacy?

Other men have said things such as:

- "I will be a more present, attentive, and emotionally mature father, and will positively affect my children's lives."

- "I will honor my spouse's needs and my own needs. I will take more responsibility in the relationship and be a better husband."

- "I will do whatever is necessary to save my marriage by taking responsibility for my part in injuring it and now rehabilitating it."

- "I will design a business around my life so I can live fully."

- "My family and co-workers will see me as a leader. My actions and interactions will be congruent with who I am."

- "I will create a positive co-parenting relationship with my former spouse and be a 100% present in my children's presence."

- "I will have a healthier, more productive relationship with money."

- "I will have other men in my life—guys who have my back—whom I trust and with whom I enjoy my time."

- I will have a mature and intimate relationship that sets me free from my old, unhealthy relationship patterns."

- I will regain my fitness, and adopt a nutritional and healthy life-style that supports my longevity."

These are all possible wins that lie ahead for you in accordance with your values, which is very important. At this stage of Your Men's Journey, your job is to imagine what's possible, and to be open to the untapped power that resides in you to make any or all of these outcomes happen. It is *not* the time to figure out how to make these outcomes happen, just to know that they are possible.

✍️ JOURNAL ENTRY #6

Using the affirmative statements listed above as a guide, take a moment to write down three to five personal win statements relative to your life and your situation(s).

Your wins will be an illuminating light to guide you—something to which you can stay connected to when times are tough. Keep these wins in a handy place where you can easily consult them, review them, and update them as you continue to learn more.

CHAPTER 4

Roadmap Step #1—Create Support for Yourself

How do you get backup?

YOU ARE HERE	Roadmap Step #1	Create Support for Yourself
	Roadmap Step #2	Speak Your Truth
	Roadmap Step #3	Declare Your Want
	Roadmap Step #4	Identify Blocks
	Roadmap Step #5	Break Through Old Ways of Being
	Roadmap Step #6	Embody Responsibility
	Roadmap Step #7	Integrate and Manifest

Mike's Story (Part 1)

Mike is a typical man who avoids asking for directions. He can do everything better himself. You know the type that doesn't ask for help? Well, this time, on the verge of divorce, Mike chose to ask.

His home life was getting worse, and Mike didn't know what to do. In passing, he mentioned his situation to a friend, who had recently gone through a divorce. The friend invited him to join a group of men who got together to talk about their lives with the common goal of becoming better men. His friend told him that some of the men were also going through marriage problems.

Mike accepted his friend's invitation. As he sat in a group of men whom he didn't know, he quickly felt at home after hearing about their struggles and victories. Many voiced similar problems and spoke about their confusion, their feelings, and their journey to be the men they were meant to be.

They too had experienced a wake-up call and were trying to figure out what it meant. They were courageous in their sharing and they told the truth. Mike could identify with just about every man there, as if each man shared a little piece of struggle that Mike was also experiencing at that moment.

Useful Things to Know

One of the biggest challenges for men is asking for help. Be sure to ask for help when it's needed and be part of the club of men willing to ask for assistance. It is male nature not to ask for help because most men think that *asking* for help is a sign of weakness and *not asking* for help is a sign of strength.

In actuality, to go at life alone is a sign of arrogance. Asking for help is a sign of strength. Fortunately, life has a way of bringing us to our knees and teaching a lesson or two in humility. Only then will we understand the concept of surrender.

For most men, it usually takes a painful event to get their attention and wake them up. Your willingness to *ask for help* and *receive help* is a huge component in being able to make something useful out of your wake-up call.

Keep in mind that you have support on Your Men's Journey while trying to answer your wake-up call. Sure, there is a tremendous feeling of being alone when you are in The Tunnel (Alison Armstrong, *Keys to the Kingdom*, PAX Programs Incorporated, 2003), and many men—just like you—are fighting the same battle.

The paradox is that, while you feel alone in The Tunnel, you are alone only when you separate yourself from the company of other men in their own tunnel (assuming you exercise your freedom of choice in joining a group). The time you spend in The Tunnel depends on who you are and how actively you take on the challenge. For some men, The Tunnel lasts for six months; for others, it lasts for years. Each man has his own set of challenges and setbacks.

The following recommended action steps will help you move forward at a pace that corresponds with how actively you want to deal with where you are. There is no required order to follow them nor is it essential that you do all of them. As you read the steps, pay attention to the ones that resonate with you and/or make you uncomfortable, and decide which one(s) are best for you.

Action Steps to Consider for Creating Support

Action Step: Join a support group

Find out about the local support groups in your area. Regardless of the nature of your wake-up call (e.g., divorce, health, money, parenting, marital challenges, or the desire for a purpose-filled life), you'll be surprised how many groups, blogs, and websites are available.

There are men's groups that exist simply for men to meet up and support each other. Often, these groups are associated with men's initiatory weekends (e.g., "Action Step: Sign up for a men's weekend," below) and are typically open to all men who commit to experiencing the weekend; however, some men's groups do not have this requirement. (For more information about men's support groups, see the Resources section.)

Action Step: Attend a workshop

Numerous workshops can address the issues of your wake-up call. (Read "Menstuff.org" in the Resources section.)

Action Step: Sign up for a men's weekend

My first experience at a men's initiation weekend rocked my world. I had no idea that men supported and cared for each other in this way. Forty men whom I didn't know—young guys, old guys, tough guys, black guys, and gay guys—supported me on my journey and paid for the right to be there. For three days, they helped me receive what I was there to achieve. They held me accountable when I strayed from my path, and they loved me the whole time.

This experience made me question everything I knew about male friends and their roles in my life. I decided that, if I had this kind of support and fierceness *with strangers*, I might have the same thing with my best guy friends.

I decided to learn how to do this, and it became a long and difficult journey. While I now have a best buddy, whom I appreciate and to whom I can openly say, "Love you, man" or "Love you, bro" in the presence of other guys, it took patience and trust to achieve this level of comfort.

Men's weekends or retreats can be a powerful and life-changing experience for many men. These weekends are a right of passage into manhood, which will serve you in many areas of your life beyond just getting through The Tunnel.

Many men speak to the desire of getting beyond talking about their issues and "doing something" about them. This is usually an indicator that the man is ready to do some healing work in the company of other men. This is a critical distinction from coaching and therapy in that it takes far more than one man to create the safe healing environment for a man to "do his work."

The initiation weekend is the place for men to have an experience that transcends talking in the company of other men who have already had or are now ready for their experience. (For more information, see "Men's Initiation Weekend" and "Menstuff.org" in the Resources section.)

Action Step: Hire a coach or therapist

Depending on the area in your life to which the wake-up call correlates, discerning between hiring a coach or therapist can be challenging.

A coach will help you set goals, deal with obstacles, and help you with accountability. An excellent coach will assist you in bringing your attention to what needs to be addressed and identifying how it's holding you back in life. A therapist will help you deal with issues such as anxiety, rage, sadness, depression, and feelings of being overwhelmed.

You may need or want the services of one or both. If you are interested in my coaching services and experience through your wake-up call, visit www.yourmensjouney.com.

Action Step: Form your own support group (We group)

You may have some good quality male friends who share a similar desire to start their journey. Talk to them about forming your own group. An easy and manageable number is three, known as a triad. Three guys with similar core values and a desire to be better men can accomplish a lot in the mutual support of each other. I call them "We groups." (More information on We groups can be found at www.yourmens-journey.com.) If you don't have close male friends to form a We group, then reading and following Chapter 17, "Real Male Friendships," would be good for you to get started.

Action Step: Do all of the above

Depending on your drive and your resources, you may want to take more than one action step. Once I got on the path of improving my life and being a better man, there was no turning back. I hired a therapist, attended a men's initiation weekend, hired a coach, and attended various workshops. (To read more about my experience, see Chapter 20, "Final Words—My Story.")

Action Step: Include the woman in your life

Talk to your wife, girlfriend, or partner about the fact that you are in The Tunnel. Alison Armstrong, author of *Keys to the Kingdom*, teaches that, because women relate by connecting, we men must be aware of this desire to connect when we answer our wake-up call. It is common for men to say nothing about what they are going through and to go into isolation.

Since men must go into The Tunnel alone, you need to inform your women that The Tunnel is temporary and you are still connected to them. If you talk to your wife, girlfriend, or partner about where you are, you can then ask her to listen to you and be your friend during this important stage in your life.

Worthwhile Wins on Which to Set Your Sights

- You will learn specific and relevant information that will help you deal with your wake-up call.

- You will receive some needed one-on-one attention, along with some necessary accountability.

- You will receive insights and tools to handle rage, sadness, depression, and anxiety so you can minimize your impact on people you love.

- You will experience trust, honesty, and truth.

- Other men will hold you accountable in a way you could never do yourself.

- You will hear and be heard by others, which will help you learn about yourself.

- Being with other men will reinforce the fact that you are not alone.

- You will gain support by staying connected to your wife, girl-friend, or partner while you are in The Tunnel.

- You will experience a deep sense of community with other men that perhaps you have wanted all your life. These various forms of support will prepare you to continue on your way, as you embark on Roadmap Step #2 of Your Men's Journey.

CHAPTER 5

Roadmap Step #2—
Speak Your Truth

What can you gain from speaking your truth to others?

✓	Roadmap Step #1	Create Support for Yourself
YOU ARE HERE	Roadmap Step #2	Speak Your Truth
	Roadmap Step #3	Declare Your Want
	Roadmap Step #4	Identify Blocks
	Roadmap Step #5	Break Through Old Ways of Being
	Roadmap Step #6	Embody Responsibility
	Roadmap Step #7	Integrate and Manifest

Mike's Story (Part 2)

When it came time for Mike to speak in the group, he felt the anxiety of having to be vulnerable in front of guys he didn't know. This was *not* something he normally did. Yet, the fact that the other guys spoke honestly gave Mike courage.

Mike shared that he was confused, angry, sad, and unsure all at the same time. He shared that he had fear about the uncertainty of his future—being without his wife, being a single dad, and being alone. He admitted that he had lots of questions he couldn't answer and, as a result, felt as if his very being was in question. The men listened and said nothing, simply giving him their attention and compassion.

About halfway through his sharing, Mike began to feel a sense of belonging, a bit of confidence, and a growing sense that things were going to be OK, no matter what was going to happen with his marriage.

When he was done, it occurred to Mike that maybe this was his time to figure out some lingering questions about who he was as a man and, more importantly, *who he wanted to be*. All this from speaking to a bunch of guys he didn't know! Mike drove home that night with a small sense of relief and a slight smile on his face. He felt more ready to take on the challenges of the next day.

Useful Things to Know

In order to navigate your wake-up call successfully, it is essential to understand and manage your feelings. Chances are that your present state of emotional literacy—and its limitations—have contributed to your wake-up call, so bringing your attention and commitment to this area is necessary now.

Having emotional literacy means accepting that you have feelings, understanding what your feelings are at any given moment, and acquiring the knowledge of how to work with your feelings. For men, this means feeling your emotions and not allowing them to "run" your life and unconsciously influence how you make decisions.

Here are some simple things to keep in mind:

- **Get interested in your emotions.** In this Roadmap Step #2, the emphasis is on *focusing internally* and *getting interested in what is true for you* in any given moment. Once you've created some support in the way that works for you (i.e., with the right individuals in the right environment), get interested in what's going on for you emotionally. Being interested is about connecting to your feelings, which are pure, unadulterated truths about yourself. If you need someone to model this for you, it's OK to ask. This isn't something modeled for most men, so it is all right to feel a bit tentative at first.

- **Your "whole truth" includes your past, your shadow beliefs, and your behaviors.** Shadow beliefs and behaviors often arise from painful incidents that happened to you, and then show up as negative beliefs that you created when you were too young to protect yourself (e.g., "I'm not good enough"). For example, your dad asked you to clean the garage and put away all the tools on the workbench. Since you were only 10 years old, you did the best you could. When he came out and saw what you did, he yelled and said that you did it wrong and that he would just have to do it himself. Not only did this scare you, but you also heard that "you were wrong," "you didn't do it well enough," and "you're not good enough." Because of this experience, you no longer offer to help, and you do things independently for fear of doing them wrong. Typically linked to these beliefs are protective behaviors that you unconsciously act out and that often cause disruption in your life and relationships. Your shadow beliefs are the parts of you that you hide, repress, and deny. You may be unaware of your shadow beliefs and behaviors, and they can get you in trouble if you don't pay attention to them. When these negative beliefs influence your behaviors, you often get less-than-desirable consequences in your relationships. Since many people have a boss or are a boss, a negative belief example would be "people are untrustworthy." The negative effect is that the boss micromanages his staff, causing them to feel patronized and not trusted, which leads to poor morale. The goal is to become aware of them, understand them and not react to them, and learn to act consciously.

- **Your truth is in your body.** Your feelings are stored in your body, not in your mind. Feelings are part of you on a cellular level. In Chapter 2, "What to Do First," I introduced the core feelings (sadness/grief, anger, joy, fear, and shame). When you go to the gym, you work certain muscle groups. In the same way, knowing and accessing your truth, and making an effort to speak it aloud, are the equivalents of strengthening muscles that you may not have used much.

The following action steps will assist you a great deal in building your emotional awareness, especially in your relationships. Getting to know yourself and speaking your truth will help bring *integrity* into your life. This is essential in Your Men's Journey.

It is best to practice your truth while speaking with your male support group until you get comfortable with it. If you are in a men's group already, the experience of hearing others speak their truth is valuable in and of itself, and taking a risk to do the same may be healing for you. If you haven't joined a men's group, it is essential that you consider doing so to experience this very important and critical step.

Remember, your truth is not limited to the data or your beliefs about what is happening to you. If you are angry, sad, or feeling shame, this is also your truth.

An example of speaking your truth might look like this: "I am angry that my wife wants a divorce. I'm afraid of what life will be like after selling the house. I'm sad that I won't be able to see my kids every day. This isn't fair and I didn't do anything to deserve this."

If speaking your truth is something you are not accustomed to doing, I recommend practicing in a setting with an experienced man whom you trust, or in a group with an experienced facilitator. This is where a coach or therapist might benefit you the most if you do not join or form a group.

Action Steps to Consider for Speaking Your Truth

Action Step: Talk to an emotionally literate close friend or mentor

You might have a close friend with whom you can share your feelings, frustrations, and life challenges, or someone whom you trust in your church, synagogue, or temple. Find that person, explain what your goal is, and begin talking to them.

Action Step: Practice speaking your truth in a group

Depending on the nature of your wake-up call, you may have chosen a men's group, a grief group, a fathering group, a career transition group, an Alcoholics Anonymous group, or some other kind of group. When you are in the group, be sure to speak up. Tell the others what your truth is, and practice saying it aloud as often as you can. You may find it helpful to write your truth on small notes and use them as reminders.

Action Step: Find a physical activity you enjoy, get in your body, and then speak

Do you often find it challenging (most men do) to get out of your head and into your body? Since feelings reside in the body, a great way to get to know them is to get physical. Grab a buddy and check in with each other about what's going on in your lives and how you feel about what's up. Whatever you are feeling, see if you can identify where in your body you are feeling the sadness/grief, anger, joy, fear or shame.

Worthwhile Wins on Which to Set Your Sights

- You may find that speaking your truth feels good! There is nothing more freeing than speaking your truth as a man. It is the cornerstone of your integrity.

- You may find that speaking your truth to others fosters trust. When you speak truthfully, others will respect and trust you more. This will become evident in all your relationships, both personal and business.

- You may find that accessing and speaking your truth creates opportunity for personal insights. This simply means you discover things about yourself when you are committed to learning something about whom and what you are.

- You may find that voicing your challenges and beliefs reduces the stronghold those feelings have over you when you put your attention on them. With this attention, you will reclaim power over your challenges and beliefs and make different choices.

Note: If you are having difficulty accessing and/or feeling your feelings, a therapist and/or men's weekend can help you kick start your emotional literacy efforts. I highly recommend a men's weekend for fast-tracking your personal journey. (For suggestions, see "Men's Initiation Weekend" and "Menstuff.org" in the Resources section.)

CHAPTER 6

Roadmap Step #3—
Declare Your Want

What is your "hot want"?

	Roadmap Step #1	Create Support for Yourself
✓	Roadmap Step #1	Create Support for Yourself
✓	Roadmap Step #2	Speak Your Truth
YOU ARE HERE	Roadmap Step #3	Declare Your Want
	Roadmap Step #4	Identify Blocks
	Roadmap Step #5	Break Through Old Ways of Being
	Roadmap Step #6	Embody Responsibility
	Roadmap Step #7	Integrate and Manifest

49

Mike's Story (Part 3)

Four weeks had gone by since Mike had the conversation with his wife about the state of their marriage. He had attended three men's support groups by that time, and had been ruminating on a question posed to him in the last support group meeting:

"What is your 'hot want'"?

Put another way, "What is the big change you want to make for the better?"

Mike initially had no idea how to answer this question. All he knew was that he was potentially facing a divorce and this question was challenging him emotionally, physically, mentally, and spiritually. Did this question have anything to do with his marriage? Was it relevant to his potential divorce? More importantly, what was the damn *answer*?

Mike was accustomed to providing basic needs and wants for his family. He rarely thought about himself first in this context. On top of this, with a divorce looming over his head, Mike felt much anxiety about the uncertainty of his future—with or without his wife. To think about what he wanted only brought up what he *didn't* want: a divorce! Yet, an inner sense of excitement stirred about the possibility of not only answering this question but actually having what he most wanted … even though he had no clue what that was.

At the next support group meeting, the leader suggested an exercise where each man would describe in detail his "hot want." He mentioned the importance of saying it aloud, which created the possibility of actually having what they wanted becoming real.

The leader said that taking their attention off the crisis, and instead focusing on the "big change" they wanted to make for the better, would actually help them move through their crisis. He shared that the specific challenge life often hands men (i.e., their wake-up call) may reveal clues about the "hot want." Last, and certainly not least, the leader mentioned that who they were as men, and who they were meant to be as men, would play a big role in getting their "hot want."

Mike gave much thought to the question posed by the leader as well as some of the things he heard his wife tell him, such as being emotionally unavailable to her and to their boys. It reminded him of watching his father with his mother and how, in some familiar way, he too longed for his dad when he was young. It was difficult for him to hear these comments from his wife. He felt sad just thinking about it and was determined to make some changes.

What Mike *really* wanted was a meaningful, strong relationship with his wife—and, if not her, then someone else. He wanted to be a better husband than his dad was to his mom. He wanted to be a great father to his two boys and improve upon his experience with his own dad.

Mike was beginning to understand deeply that, to do these things, he had to transcend some old ways of being and become a much more mature and responsible man in his roles as father and husband. He sensed this more mature man would serve him in his business, too. As the owner of his business, he was regarded as a leader. *Who would this new man be?*

Mike knew that, in order to make this transition, many changes would have to occur. He would have to take a serious look at himself, and find out what was getting in his way to being this "man he wanted to be" in his roles as husband, father, leader, and businessman. He could sense this new direction as well as sense something blocking him. He was determined to find out what it was.

Useful Things to Know

Whether it's a health or death scare of a loved one, your own health scare, a divorce, financial ruin, out-of-balance work and life, or even your own recognition of a purposeless life, this event—your wake-up call—has happened in your life for a reason. It's here to get your attention. It's calling the man you are meant to be to step up and show himself.

In my coaching and facilitating experiences, I have noticed that most men need to be bonked on the head (usually with the metaphorical Volkswagen) in order for them to want to make any significant change. The connection I want you to make here is that stepping into the man you are meant to be is *correlated directly* to you getting what you want most in life. The two go hand in hand.

Often, the pain of your wake-up call and your experience of that pain are the main drivers in your desire to make a big change in your life. Many men go into reaction, and then work hard to make sure they avoid whatever happened (e.g., a divorce or a job loss) in the future. Examples of this behavior include pretending it didn't happen, using alcohol and drugs, or simply vowing never to take a risk again. Unfortunately, these behaviors are about not wanting to feel pain. They are not about facing the crisis and doing something about it.

Still, the pain is what makes your want "hot." The burning part of your want is the fresh pain associated with how things didn't turn out, and your mind telling you that it could happen again. This is why stepping into the man you are capable of being is so important. You are going to have to confront what got in the way of you having what you want … and, in most instances, *it was you.*

Want a fulfilling and intimate marriage? Focus on being the man you are meant to be. Want to be a great dad? Want to be a great leader in life and business? Guess what? The answer is to focus on being the man you are meant to be.

I am not telling you to be like other great men. Being the man *you* want to be means being the man *you say you are* ... by your own design. This will require courage, will, commitment, and a positive attitude.

Roadmap Step #3 is shifting your attention away from your wake-up call and towards what big change for the better you want to make in your life. By taking this step, you create a positive, personal context (or meaningful reason) to pull yourself through and out of your crisis (which, by now, I invite you to view as a "gift" of sorts).

Inside each of us is a source of power. This power has always been there and is available to you. It is a power of focus, and "masculine focus" is part of who you are as a man. In conjunction with this power of focus lies a source of vitality inside you: the "state of being strong and active." You will need this vitality in conjunction with your focus to identify your "hot want" and make it happen.

✍️ JOURNAL ENTRY #7

What is your masculine focus?

The following action steps are an opportunity to bring together your vitality, focus, and vision for the man you want to be, so you can formulate your "hot want" statement for the rest of the Roadmap steps. The questions in these action steps give you different vantage points to look at the big change you want to make.

Some men take the easy road and simply focus on a potential win. I'm suggesting that it's harder to look at your life honestly, acknowledge the wake-up call as a result of how you have been living your life, and then craft your "hot want" from that place. Doing it this way is certainly more challenging, and it's the most rewarding.

You decide. The choice is yours.

Action Steps to Consider for Declaring Your Want

Action Step: Go back to your potential wins

 JOURNAL ENTRY #8

From "The Light at the End of the Tunnel" (Chapter 3, "Starting Your Journey"), list your top three win statements from Journal Entry #6 by order of priority. What's most pressing and important to you?

Action Step: Review your answers

 JOURNAL ENTRY #9

From "See What Is: Confronting Hard Truths" (Chapter 3, "Starting Your Journey"), list three from the list of Seven Reality Checkpoints that challenge you the most and hold the most room for improvement. Which areas are most pressing now? Notice the discomfort and perhaps even pain associated with looking at these areas. Take note of the hardest area to view—it may just be the one area around which you need to shift and change your beliefs.

Action Step: Make one list (combining win statements with reality checkpoints) from the above two action steps

---

 JOURNAL ENTRY #10

Do your wins align with the areas that hold the most room for improvement? Simply notice the potential relationship between the two. What area of masculine focus do you want to address?

Action Step: Create your "hot want" statement

✍ JOURNAL ENTRY #11

Plug in the appropriate phrase and terms:

"As a better (husband, partner, single man, father, leader, friend)

_____,

I want to create _____, so

that I can _____."

Here are some examples:

- "As a better *father*, I want to create a better relationship with my two sons, so I can positively influence their lives and mine."

- "As a better *leader*, I want to model accountability, personal responsibility, and collaboration with my team and employees, so I can effectively bring out the leader in each of them."

- "As a better *husband*, I want to bring my vitality, authenticity, and integrity to our relationship, honoring my spouse and myself, so we both can enjoy intimacy and personal growth."

- "As a *maturing masculine single man*, I want to bring my masculinity, power, heart, and confidence into a conscious relationship, so I can create a fulfilling, mature, and evolving partnership."

- "As a *physically healthy man*, I want to create an exercise and nutrition program that promotes inner and outer strength, so I can experience the fullness of my life without physical limitations."

Worthwhile Wins on Which to Set Your Sights

- You will get clarity around the big change that you want to make in your life.

- You will get an idea as to the type of man you will need to be to make it happen.

- You will experience a higher mood level (fueled by possibilities) to aid you in facing your present challenge.

- You will acquire a positive personal reason that can act as a guiding light for your path.

- You will get more in touch with your true masculine essence and its power of focus.

- You will find more confidence.

- You will receive inspiration and hope.

CHAPTER 7

Your Father

What does your father have to do with your present situation?

You're Like Him

What does your father have to do with you and your present situation? *A lot.* We men are a lot like our fathers—warts and all. Even if you don't like it, you watched how your father (or male equivalent) lived his life and it became your frame of reference. That's the way it works. If you embrace this difficult truth, you will have a much easier time on your own path of becoming the man you are meant to be.

Put simply, your father was the first male model you ever had, and those admirable qualities (as well as his less-than-admirable traits) rubbed off on you. Even if you didn't grow up with a dad, you had a model—maybe it was a coach, an uncle, a grandpa, or even a stepdad. Perhaps you had a supermom trying to *be* a dad. Either way, this person had a major influence in your life.

Here you are, a growing man, and you've made some choices. Maybe you've chosen to emulate your father (and have succeeded to some degree) or maybe you've sworn to yourself that you're "never going to be like him" (and have succeeded to some degree with that, too). Either way, your father is still present in how you live your life, whether you admire him or rebel against him.

Do you have any pain associated with the memories of your father and his behaviors? What did you do with the memories of those pains? The answer for most men is they buried those memories and feelings, and they still live deeply inside of them. How deep are these feelings for you?

Whether you like it or not, your experiences with your father shaped your beliefs. Some of these beliefs are conscious (such as how a man should act) and some of them are not (such as whether you are loveable and what you may and won't do). Still, your learned beliefs and behaviors are always there and, if you are not aware of them, they operate unmonitored in your relationships, often to the detriment of others and yourself.

You have to uncover these patterns and beliefs because you want to understand your father's model of the world to be a better father, husband, leader, and friend. You can't move forward in life as a conscious man until you can acknowledge that you are like your father, even in the ways you wish to reject.

The Five Fatherly Influences

Every father influences his son in five distinct ways. These Five Fatherly Influences cover the range of basic information (such as what it means to be a man) to the specifics of dealing with other men, handling feelings, dealing with women, and handling money.

As you read about the Five Fatherly Influences, take your time to observe how your father's influences are present in your life. Strive to remember as much as you can, answer the questions as completely as you can, and write down your answers so you can refer to them later.

I invite you to view this chapter as one of the most important chapters in the book because it will give you the opportunity to learn about what imprinting you received from your father or male equivalent.

Some of what happened to you was good and some of it wasn't. Bringing your attention to the not-so-good stuff will give you power over it instead of it having power over your behavior and your life. This personal information is the key to making a different (and conscious) set of choices in your life.

> *Old man look at my life,*
> *I'm a lot like you were.*
> *Old man look at my life,*
> *I'm a lot like you were.*
> *Love lost, such a cost,*
> *Give me things that don't get lost.*
> *Like a coin that won't get tossed*
> *Rolling home to you.*
>
> —Neil Young, "Old Man," from *Harvest*, 1972

Fatherly Influence #1: How your dad demonstrated what it meant to be a man

When you were just a little guy, you watched and listened to your father, stepfather, or other male figure. You watched the things he did, and it had a huge impact on your subconscious brain and your behavior. You watched how he treated people, how he treated your sister (or brother), and how he treated your mom. You may have seen his relationship with your great grandparents or grandparents.

You watched him work to provide for his family (or not) and, when it was time for you to pick a career and provide for your family, your dad's work ethic was on your mind. You watched your father every day.

Maybe there was no central male figure in your life on a regular basis and you witnessed coaches or other men who had qualities of what it meant to be a man.

Watching these men shaped your view of what a man is.

To the extent that this serves you, great; to the extent that it doesn't, you are not alone. The below questions are intended to raise your awareness, so you can notice how influential your father has been on who you are as a man, and decide for yourself what kind of man *you* want to be. The path to doing this in a positive way requires you to become fully aware of your father's influences, both good and bad, so you can better know yourself as a man.

Take the time, eliminate any distractions, and write down the answers to the following questions in your journal:

✍️ JOURNAL ENTRY #12

What characteristics do you recall about your father that defined him as a man? You can reference the masculine core values questions (Journal Entries #2 through 5) from Chapter 3, "Starting Your Journey."

✍️ JOURNAL ENTRY #13

What characteristics from your father play a part in who you are as a man today?

🖎 JOURNAL ENTRY #14

What "old school" characteristics about your father have you rejected?

🖎 JOURNAL ENTRY #15

What qualities did you create in opposition to your father's "old school" characteristics? *Don't skip this question!*

Be patient with your answers. When you can acknowledge these hidden and rejected parts of yourself, and can admit that you are like your father, you have taken a huge leap in stepping into the man you are meant to be.

🖎 JOURNAL ENTRY #16

What good qualities did your father pass down to you?

🖎 JOURNAL ENTRY #17

With the answers to Journal Entries #14 and #15, try to list some positive qualities of what it means to be a man by *your* standards. (Hint: These qualities may often be the opposite of what you rejected from your father or what was absent and needed.)

Fatherly Influence #2: How your one-on-one relationship with your father laid the foundation of how you relate to other men

Your father (or male equivalent) was the first experience in relating to a male, which imprinted you and shaped how you interact with men even today.

If your father was like most men of his era, he may have been unavailable emotionally (or an alcoholic, or both). If you and your father had lots of talks, and he encouraged you and shared his true feelings, you are a lucky man. If you didn't have a dominant male figure in your life, relating to men will be shaped by the absence of this male experience.

If there was no emotional connection between you and your dad, chances are that you still carry the pain of that disconnection. If your father told you one thing and then did another, you may have learned not to trust the words he spoke. If your father drank or raged, his anger may have taught you to always be on the watch.

In order to protect yourself, you likely created behaviors to numb the pain of the disconnection. You probably decided to keep your distance and not try to get close. As a grown man, these experiences typically manifest in a lack of trust for men and having few, if any, relationships with men of any significance.

You may have rationalized your father's behavior by deciding something was wrong with *you*—that you weren't enough, weren't lovable, or didn't (and still don't) matter. This normal survival behavior happens unconsciously.

The resulting unconscious beliefs you hold about yourself play a significant role in how you relate to men. If you experienced physical, mental, or verbal abuse at the hands of your father, you've had to carry even more pain. If you avoid these wounds, the pain in your life increases as well as the likelihood that you will pass these beliefs and behaviors to your children, or perpetrate your pain on your loved ones.

Put another way, most men share these emotional pains—more men than you could ever realize. Still, the first step is to acknowledge what you learned from your father, and realize how this relationship formed deep beliefs.

Bringing awareness to your wounds (as opposed to denying them) is the way out and up. *What you do next is up to you.* Whether you hire a therapist, attend a men's weekend, work with a coach, or go to a men's group with a skilled facilitator, you have plenty of options other than deny-ing it and allowing it to ruin your life and the lives of those around you.

Your dad was your "first man" (i.e., your first model of a male rela-tionship was you and your dad). The nature, frequency, and depth of that relationship when you were young all play a big role in how you relate (or don't relate) to men in your life.

As part of your journey to answer your wake-up call, I invite you to answer the following questions in order to raise your awareness. Notice what feelings come up in the course of this experience and journal your answers. Some of them are Yes/No questions and others require some thought.

✍ JOURNAL ENTRY #18

How did your father relate to you? Was he present with you or distracted?

✍ JOURNAL ENTRY #19

What type of conversations did you have with your father?

✍ JOURNAL ENTRY #20

Did your father do things with you? What did you do together?

✍ JOURNAL ENTRY #21

Did your father tell you he loved you?

✍ JOURNAL ENTRY #22

Did your father play with you when you were young?

🖎 JOURNAL ENTRY #23

What did you want your father to say and/or do that he didn't (or couldn't)?

🖎 JOURNAL ENTRY #24

Was your father jealous of other men and their successes?

🖎 JOURNAL ENTRY #25

How did your father talk about other men?

🖎 JOURNAL ENTRY #26

How do your father's behaviors show up in your male relationships?

🖎 JOURNAL ENTRY #27

Do you desire to repeat any of these behaviors with your children? Are you repeating any of these behaviors with your children?

Fatherly Influence #3: How your dad dealt with his feelings

How your father did (or didn't) experience his feelings taught you how you deal with yours. If your dad didn't deal with feelings in the moment, and stuffed them down like most men do, chances are that, in your adult life, you experience the outburst or sideways version of feelings, where things "bubble up" and "pop out" in surprising ways. Perhaps you simply keep a low profile or maybe you don't experience many feelings at all. Either way, your dad showed you what "a man" does with feelings.

When it comes to being an adult man, a decent amount of emotional literacy (even if you weren't taught it) will go a long way in improving the qualities of your relationships, your career, and your life in general.

For this reason, I strongly encourage you to explore and commit to your own emotional literacy as you step into being the man you are meant to be. Men are people, and people feel—sometimes a lot. Becoming familiar with your emotions and understanding how you experience them are nonnegotiable steps as you move forward. After all, emotional intelligence has become a popular subject that is gaining relevance in the business world.

Here are some shortcuts to get you started. The feelings men stuff (or repress) most often are sadness/grief, anger, fear, and shame. The problem with stuffing your feelings is they eventually find their way out—verbally, physically, or both—or find their way in (as in the case of shame) and slowly burn away at your sense of well-being.

Unconscious anger often violently manifests outward as a result of inner feelings of sadness, fear, or grief/loss. Unacknowledged shame often manifests as a violent inner reaction to yourself in reaction to sadness, fear, or grief/loss. Put another way, anger is fear or sadness/grief felt but not expressed the moment you feel it. Because it's buried, it festers; when it finally gets to the surface, it shows up as anger.

In order to learn about your own expression/suppression of feelings, I encourage you to use the following questions about your father to reflect on what you may have learned from him.

✍ JOURNAL ENTRY #28

How did your father show his feelings?

JOURNAL ENTRY #29

What feelings did your father show?

 JOURNAL ENTRY #30

What did your dad do when he got mad? Did he yell? Did he get seethingly silent? Did he leave?

 JOURNAL ENTRY #31

How do you deal with your own anger? Do you yell? Do you get silent? Do you leave?

I offer the following process, learned from Mondo Zen, to help you shift from reacting to responding. (For more information, see "Silent Meditation Retreat and Emotional Koan Work" in the Resources section.) By getting curious about your anger when you feel it arise, you can take the "charge" out of it and make different choices about how you respond.

The next time you are angry, try the following exercise and ask these questions:

- What is true about your anger? Are you afraid? Are you sad? Are you grieving a loss? Notice the answers and acknowledge them. When the underlying truth of anger is sadness, fear, or grief/loss, a core caring exists about you or someone else, or something has been scratched, irritated, or threatened, and you often don't know how to acknowledge the hurt without reacting.

The following questions will aid you in getting out of reaction and into the source of your hurt.

- Who or what do you really care about? In instances where the underlying truth of your anger is fear, then an appropriate response might be to protect yourself or your loved ones. When the underlying truth is sadness/grief, then acknowledging whom or what you really care about may be all you need to do. If this place of sadness/grief could talk, what would it say to you?

- Notice your answer to the above question, "Who or what do you really care about?" and acknowledge it. Do you notice the difference of how it feels when you answer the question around caring versus the actual feeling of anger? This difference is the fundamental difference between reacting versus responding.

- If you were angry as a result of what someone else did or said, what might you say to them from a perceived place of caring?

- What might be different for you and them regarding how each of you feel towards each other? How might the other person talk back to you? Consider how you might respond to that person given what you now know.

Fatherly Influence #4: How your father related to your mom

What you saw your father do influences how you relate to women. Like most men, your first exposure to witnessing a man and a woman relate to each other occurred in your home.

It may have been your mom and dad, your stepmom or stepdad, your grandparents, or your dad and his girlfriend. How your father respected the woman in his life, how he spoke to her, listened to her, and touched her all play a role in shaping how you are with women.

When it came to disagreements, the way your father acted relative to your mom is also important to note. Whether your father demonstrated love with words, physical affection, acts of service, gifts, spending time, or not at all, it influenced how you relate to women.

You may have a dark side to what you saw. You may have seen some behaviors from your father that you abhorred and resolved never to repeat. Remember the suggestion to embrace the notion, "You are like your dad, warts and all!" This is one of those times.

Most young boys who witness verbal, physical, or emotional abuse by their father towards their mother are often limited as to what they can do to protect their mother. Did you experience pain due to your helplessness? The feeling may be worse if your dad shot you down when you attempted to rescue your mom and failed.

If this describes your experience, the boy in you represses this feeling of helplessness that may come out later in life, typically in a similar form of abuse towards the woman in your life, or you may act helpless around women.

You might have felt scared, angry, or sad after witnessing your father treat your mom in a negative way. It might have hurt you emotionally and, in an instant, you decided not to be like him. All of this may have happened unconsciously as you buried both the event and your decisions and didn't fully experience the emotions that were happening for you at the time (e.g., helplessness, sadness/grief, fear, or anger).

Fast forward to the present, and imagine a scenario with a woman in your life. She may be your wife. She may be your daughter. She might even be your boss. You may be repeating history by acting like your father or by acting in the extreme opposite way. It's important to recognize that, *either way,* you are in reaction.

For example, many men with whom I've worked often witnessed their fathers belittling their mothers. As a child, they vowed never to do this; however, as an adult, they belittle their wives—even *if they don't want to.* They say that it's a reflex. Recognizing they are imitating what they were taught helps break the cycle to make a new choice. If you don't know, you won't change your behavior.

By noticing that you are acting like your father (or creating the exact opposite behavior), you may make a conscious choice to respond "pro-actively" from your adult heart versus your childish developed response.

This is an opportunity to become aware of these handed-down behaviors and realize how they don't serve you in your interactions with women. From this place of awareness, you can choose a new way to relate to women that is not associated with your dad or your past behavior.

When you choose *your own way* of responding, possible outcomes you may experience are improved intimacy and communication with your wife or girlfriend, and healthy modeling for your sons and daughters or a female superior, who actively supports you at work because she is no longer the target of your defiant behavior.

I encourage you to take some time to answer the following questions to help you examine your father's influence on how you relate to women, both consciously and unconsciously.

✍️ JOURNAL ENTRY #32

How did your dad treat your mom (or stepmom or girlfriend)? Did he treat her with respect?

✍️ JOURNAL ENTRY #33

Did your father honor your mother? If so, how?

✍️ JOURNAL ENTRY #34

How did your father (or male equivalent) conduct himself in disagreements with your mother?

JOURNAL ENTRY #35

Is there any connection to how you relate to your wife and/or daughter that is similar or opposite to how your dad related to your mother and/or sister?

 JOURNAL ENTRY #36

Notice and acknowledge the feelings that accompany what you recall. If you did something differently, what would be a more loving approach?

Fatherly Influence #5: How your dad dealt with money and influenced your views and relationship with money

Here are several areas to review about your relationship with money.

Analyzing Your Net Worth and Self-Worth

Most of your beliefs and behaviors around money are driven and shaped from experiences you had and observations you made in the household in which you grew up. From these experiences, you etched limiting beliefs in your subconscious, and they play out in your life in various ways, such as spending, saving, earning, managing, and investing. These beliefs are often a result of your mother and father's interactions, avoidances, failures, shortcomings and teachings about money, and your family experiences with money that affected you.

Around the time of adolescence, you (like most people) awakened to the concept of economic difference. This is when you began to comprehend that some people had more money than your family, and your family had more money than other families.

Consider these possibilities:

- Maybe most of your friends came from families with money and yours didn't have much, which felt shameful.

- Maybe you tried to hide your family's economic reality because you were embarrassed.

- Maybe your family had lots of money and that was embarrassing because your friends came from families that had less money.

Regardless, instances like these can be painful in adolescence to the point of confusion, leading you to conclude that who you are as a person is related to having (or not having) money. Your life patterns around money become embedded beliefs at a cellular level as you grew and matured through life.

This unnecessary intertwining of self-worth and net worth is one root of money issues. People unconsciously resolve to make sure things will be different when they are older. This "resolving" takes the form of unconscious limiting beliefs and behaviors, which actually *reinforce the dysfunctional connection* between net worth and self-worth. Do you want to dissolve this connection?

To learn more about your unconscious money beliefs and behaviors, take some time to look intently at your family money history.

✍ JOURNAL ENTRY #37

What was your perception of your parents' economic situation?

✍ JOURNAL ENTRY #38

Did you harbor any feelings of shame or resentment towards your parents if they were poor? If they were affluent?

✍️ JOURNAL ENTRY #39

Whether your parents were affluent or poor, did you hide this from anyone as you grew up?

✍️ JOURNAL ENTRY #40

Whether your parents were affluent or poor, how did this affect your behavior around kids with more or less wealth?

✍️ JOURNAL ENTRY #41

What decisions did you make about who you are as a person as it relates to money?

Examining Your Views about Earning Money

Do you recall your father's work ethic around earning money? Depending on your upbringing, this may have shaped how you approached earning money for yourself, especially when considering being financially independent. It is important to bring your attention to how these lessons around earning money affect you.

✍️ JOURNAL ENTRY #42

Did your father's need to earn money limit his time with you, causing you to resent him (and the notion of earning money)?

✍️ JOURNAL ENTRY #43

Did your father's capacity to earn money inspire you?

 **JOURNAL ENTRY #44**

Did your father teach you about earning money?

 **JOURNAL ENTRY #45**

What money lessons did you learn from your father?

Analyzing Your Patterns for Saving Money

Saving money (or not) is another area where your father influenced you. Saving money requires vision for a financial goal in the future and discipline to save money in order to make it happen.

When it came time to save for vacations, retirement, college, and other financial goals, how did your dad or family model savings? How you approach saving money today is typically an outgrowth of your exposure to saving money when growing up. These experiences play a large role in shaping how you are today with the discipline of saving money.

Take the time, eliminate any distractions, and write down the answers to the following questions in your journal:

JOURNAL ENTRY #46

Was your dad a saver?

JOURNAL ENTRY #47

Did he ever talk to you about saving money for a "rainy day"?

JOURNAL ENTRY #48

Did your dad spend money as soon as he made it?

✎ **JOURNAL ENTRY #49**

What did you learn from your father about saving money?

Managing and Investing Money

One school of thought about managing money has to do with making sure the bills are paid, the lights stay on, the checkbook balances, and the taxes are paid. To put it humorously, managing money has to do with seeing to it that there is not "too much month at the end of the money."

Spending, saving, and earning all affect your ability to manage money. Whether your parents managed money behind the scenes or out in the open, the method in which your father and mother handled these tasks shaped how you manage your finances.

If your parents did not model money management for you, and you lived in a house of financial chaos, all you know may be the finer points of living paycheck to paycheck. You may find yourself vowing never to live like that again, and steadfastly organizing your life in a different way.

Either way, the discipline of investing money is often the most elusive area around money. Investing requires a disciplined adherence to saving money and tying it to some future goal. You could have witnessed a successful father invest for the future (for things like your college education or his retirement), you could have had a father who didn't understand investing, or you could have had a dad who "tried his luck" and didn't succeed.

Whatever the experience was, it shaped you to some degree. Take a moment to recall your father's background in investing to see where you may be repeating history.

 JOURNAL ENTRY #50

What did you learn from your father about investing?

 JOURNAL ENTRY #51

If you witnessed your father succeed in investing, did you make any decisions about investing as a result of his success?

 JOURNAL ENTRY #52

If you observed your father fail, what decision if any did you make about investing as a result of his failure?

 JOURNAL ENTRY #53

What did your father share with you about investing, and how do you think this affects your current view on it (i.e., your ability to invest)?

Spending Money

Spending habits are modeled in the home. A father may model working hard, providing for his family, and buying nothing for himself. In this example, your father modeled a martyr, and he may have passed this pattern down to you.

If a father sees himself as a martyr, resentment builds and may leak out on the children or spouse. A father can spend the majority of his money on himself to the detriment of his family, causing resentment in a child and often creating low self-worth in his children. A father can shower his loved ones with material goods in lieu of quality time, affection, and words; in fact, the family just wants his attention.

All of this may have been very confusing, painful, and even potentially lonely to you as a young boy. From a self-worth perspective, a young boy wants love and attention from his father. He wants his dad to be proud of him and see him for who he is.

If a father gives his family nonmonetary things, the child might confuse spending (or not spending) with love and attention. From a net-worth perspective (i.e., spending habits), a father may model unhealthy financial habits that a boy might continue in his adulthood. Your father may have become, or maybe still is, reactive when others close to him spend money.

Without an awareness of how your father's spending habits contributed to your emotional well-being, and how certain beliefs and behaviors took shape when you were a child, you may have missed the way in which these patterns became the norm in your adulthood. If these patterns go unchecked and lie hidden out of your consciousness, they may cause anxiety, pain, anguish, and disconnection with others.

✍ JOURNAL ENTRY #54

What do you recall about your father's spending habits?

✍ JOURNAL ENTRY #55

Did he spend money on himself very often?

✍ JOURNAL ENTRY #56

How did your father arrange for you to get spending money?

✍ JOURNAL ENTRY #57

What did he teach you about spending?

✍ JOURNAL ENTRY #58

What did your father say was a "waste of money"?

✍ JOURNAL ENTRY #59

Did he just give you money or did he make you earn it?

✍ JOURNAL ENTRY #60

Did he buy things for you above and beyond the essentials?

✍ JOURNAL ENTRY #61

If your father worked a lot and was financially affluent, what did you receive more: money or his attention?

✍ JOURNAL ENTRY #62

What father-related beliefs do you have around money that live with you today?

Interacting with Your Mother around Money

Watching your dad and mom deal with each other on the topic of money (e.g., earning, saving, managing/investing, and spending) took on a life of its own. Simply put, your father's upbringing and the influences from *his* dad and mom around money came toe to toe with your mom's influences from *her* parents around money.

When these two influences collide, families may experience heated arguments, fiery divorces, or peaceful partnerships to joint financial success stories. It is *extremely important* for you to be aware of what you noticed and learned from watching them.

If you decide to get married (or are already married), your notion of what is "right" in terms of how you relate to your spouse around money is strongly shaped by what you saw as a kid, so be aware of these influences and make your choices accordingly.

✍ JOURNAL ENTRY #63

Did your father and mother have different views on spending and saving?

✍ JOURNAL ENTRY #64

When and if they did have different views, how did they resolve their differences?

✍ JOURNAL ENTRY #65

How did your father conduct himself in disagreements with your mother around money?

✍ JOURNAL ENTRY #66

Based on what you witnessed between your father and mother around money, are there any behaviors you decided to emulate or reject?

✍ JOURNAL ENTRY #67

How do these father-based beliefs exist in your present-day relationships?

✍ JOURNAL ENTRY #68

What are the consequences of these beliefs?

 JOURNAL ENTRY #69

As it relates to watching your father and mother interact around money, what did you learn as a result and/or in spite of these interactions?

 JOURNAL ENTRY #70

Even though you might not necessarily want to admit it, how are you *like* your father when it comes to money?

 JOURNAL ENTRY #71

If you admit that you are like your father, whom does this unhealthy behavior affect?

 JOURNAL ENTRY #72

What are the negative consequences of this unhealthy behavior to you?

 JOURNAL ENTRY #73

What are the negative consequences of this unhealthy behavior to others?

 JOURNAL ENTRY #74

What would a more productive behavior look like?

 JOURNAL ENTRY #75

What might be the positive results of that productive behavior?

 JOURNAL ENTRY #76

What kind of man do you need to be to make this change?

Your Mother

What does your mother have to do with your present situation?

The Three Motherly Influences

Your mother (or female caregiver in your life) influenced you in many ways that you probably haven't considered. I invite you to learn about these influences and discover where and how they show up in your life today.

Exploring these influences may improve your relationships with women. It may help you in your relationship with your daughter, if you have one, and even unlock who you are meant to be as a man.

Awareness of your mother's influences will give you keen insights about how you relate to women, your own sense of masculinity as it relates to women (and men), your approach to intimacy and self-love, and your relationship with money.

Your experience with your mother was central to your development. Your mother may have given you all the love you needed and more (i.e., too much) or she may not have been able to give you what you needed. You may have developed certain behaviors to get love. You may have given your power away just so you could get love from your mother. You may have felt you always needed to protect her, and that is how you may have stayed connected.

I invite you to consider that part of your masculine anatomy—in particular, your testicles (aka your "balls")—is where your power metaphorically resides. You may have heard the saying, "He doesn't have any balls." This simply means that he gave his power away at an early age and doesn't stand up for himself today. This may have happened for a good reason when he was young.

As a grown man, you may be repeating any or all of these childhood patterns with an important woman in your life. These patterns may have even caused you the grief of divorce and/or consistent relationship failure.

Your relationship with your mother can affect your life in many ways—positively and negatively. I offer some perspectives to raise your awareness of your mother's influence in your life. Men typically have to address these common areas as they travel their paths to becoming the men they are capable of becoming.

Motherly Influence #1: How your mother affected your power as a man

Did you give your power away to your mother when you were a young boy? Why are family power dynamics important? Often, the key to unlocking your masculinity, and bringing it to all you do, means tapping your internal power, fortitude, conviction, and willingness to take risks. In the absence of this power, men are often passive in their lives and relationships. Focusing on where your power might lie, who has it, and what you can do to get it back are important parts of this exploration.

Many young boys with no father around them unknowingly give their power to their mom at a young age to avoid upsetting her. To the young boy, who is naturally dependent on his mother, upsetting her is a fate worse than death. It is also common for young boys to witness their fathers giving their power to their wives, thus modeling unhealthy male behavior. Were you this young boy?

By working hard at never making your mom mad, you effectively agreed to keep your mouth shut, stuff down your needs and feelings, and do whatever it took to keep the peace. Yet, later in life, you became a man and found out that the power in your balls now resides with your mother. As an adult man, you don't know how to stand up for yourself or have access to a necessary personal vitality. This transference of power from boy to mother is known in psychology as "emasculation." Maybe it happened to you.

It happened to me.

If you gave your power to your mother, you have likely repeated this pattern in your relationships with women. Rather than stand in your grounded masculine power, you cave in to please your woman, or you become so attentive to her needs and wants that you lose your own self in the process, while constantly wanting her praise and affirmation. This is a complete turnoff for women and, as any woman will tell you, "I'm not your mother!" Even if you haven't given your balls away, you may have adopted a different strategy with women by picking someone you can completely control.

Either way, your relationship with your mother is still present in your other relationships.

More importantly, your mother's influence affects the way you answer your wake-up call. When you are on a quest like this one, *you need your masculine power* to keep moving and pushing through potential obstacles.

Getting to your core truth and healing yourself is hard work, and harder work awaits you in speaking your truth. You may have a strong wife (with traits similar to your mother), who might be accustomed to *not being challenged* by a man. She may be used to having the last say or not being subject to questioning.

Consider that there is a higher probability she will respect and trust you more, and possibly even feel safer, when you begin to exhibit new behaviors around speaking your truth, standing your ground, and being willing to disagree with her.

If this rings true, here are some questions for you to answer:

- Are you afraid of your wife's (or girlfriend's) anger?

- Do you avoid upsetting your wife when you do things for yourself?

- Do you often ask for your wife's opinion on personal things when it comes to your self-image?

- Do you experience an inability to make decisions, even if it means upsetting your wife or girlfriend?

- Did you have a strong-minded, energetic, and assertive mother?

If the idea of giving away your personal power to women resonates with you, the Mankind Project's initiatory weekend for men, where I did some of my best learning, is excellent. I first started as a participant and later became part of the staff to support other men. Still, my first men's weekend was all about taking back what I had unknowingly given to my mother (my power) and it changed my life. (For men's organizations offering different themes and topics, see "Menstuff.org" in the Resources section.)

You need your masculine power to answer your wake-up call and become the man you want to be. If you are having trouble accessing your power, it is imperative that you do something about it. If you are not having trouble in this area, it is still worthwhile to examine your mother's influence and discover how it might be playing out in your life.

Take the time, eliminate any distractions, and write down the answers to the following questions in your journal:

🖉 JOURNAL ENTRY #77

Did you have a strong mother with whom you were reluctant to disagree while growing up?

🖉 JOURNAL ENTRY #78

What did you learn to do when she was upset with you? How did you deal with her being upset with you?

🖉 JOURNAL ENTRY #79

What do you remember about your mother's anger? Did she give you a look? Did she yell? Did she dismiss you outright? Did she get physical with you?

🖉 JOURNAL ENTRY #80

How did you avoid your mother's anger?

🖉 JOURNAL ENTRY #81

Did your father act passively when disagreeing with your mother? How did he respond when disagreeing with her?

JOURNAL ENTRY #82

How did your mother act towards your father when disagreeing with him? Was she dismissive? Did she have to have the last say?

JOURNAL ENTRY #83

How much of what you are discovering now is similar to your current marriage and/or prior relationships?

JOURNAL ENTRY #84

What happens to you inside when your wife (or girlfriend or female co-worker or boss) gets angry? Do you avoid speaking your truth and voicing what's important to you because of her potential reaction?

JOURNAL ENTRY #85

How does your mother having your balls (power) play out in your current relationships?

JOURNAL ENTRY #86

How does a lack of power limit you in your pursuits?

JOURNAL ENTRY #87

If you are in a relationship, have you given your power (your balls) to your woman? If so, do you want your power back?

JOURNAL ENTRY #88

Are you willing to do whatever it takes to get your balls back and live in your masculine power? What might you begin to do differently?

Motherly Influence #2: How your mother related to you and influenced how you relate to women

Understanding your mother's influence is especially important if your wake-up call is about your relationship with women. Maybe you are going through a divorce or have never been in a successful intimate relationship, and maybe you want a life partner. Maybe you have a daughter and you want to be a better model for her. Maybe you have sons and you want to protect them from your "stuff." Regardless of your motivation, looking at your relationship with your mother will give you insights into your own behavior.

It's likely that your first experience relating to a woman was with your mother or female caregiver (e.g., stepmom, grandma, aunt, or older sister). This experience formed your impressions of women—how to talk with them, how to be in a relationship with them, how to receive love, how to listen, and how to behave with women in times of conflict.

Maybe you learned some valuable lessons that you use today. Maybe some of your experiences affected you negatively and, as a result, you made unconscious decisions about your worthiness—whether you matter, are "enough," or are lovable.

Alternatively, your mom may have hurt you emotionally and colored your current view of women. Because of your past and unresolved hurt around your relationship with your mother, you may unknowingly relate to women in a way that hurts the ones you love most. Some psychologists call the emotional effects of your relationship with your mother a "mother wound."

This term might be startling to you. It is worth considering the difference between a wound with a scar and a wound you can heal. It is valuable as a man to be aware of the possibility for healing if you have an emotional wound. Until you heal this wound, you often hurt those around you who unconsciously remind you of your past hurts—often your spouse or girlfriend and sometimes your daughters.

Everything you have learned—consciously and unconsciously—comes into play when you are in a relationship with a woman. Think about it, and then answer the following questions:

- How have your girlfriends been like your mother?

- How have they been different?

- How is what you learned from your mother playing into your current relationships?

- Where do you see your mother's influence (positively and negatively)?

- How do the women with whom you interact trigger your mother wounds?

After the "love dust" wears off, the woman standing before you is certain to spark unresolved issues with your mother.

Your work as a man on the path to being a better man and husband is to heal these wounds and *avoid* projecting them onto your wife, daughter, or females in the workplace. Part of your work requires you to answer the questions below with honesty and courage.

✍🏽 JOURNAL ENTRY #89

Was your mother overprotective, or did she cut you enough slack and allow you to make mistakes?

✍🏽 JOURNAL ENTRY #90

If your mother was overprotective, how did you handle those situations?

✍ JOURNAL ENTRY #91

What did you need from your mother that you struggled to express?

✍ JOURNAL ENTRY #92

Did you feel supported by your mother or did you feel like you were a burden?

✍ JOURNAL ENTRY #93

What behaviors did you develop to get what you needed?

✍ JOURNAL ENTRY #94

How did your mother show affection towards you?

✍ JOURNAL ENTRY #95

Was the affection what you wanted?

✍ JOURNAL ENTRY #96

What behaviors did you use to get what you needed?

✍ JOURNAL ENTRY #97

Was your mother emotionally available or emotionally absent? If she was emotionally absent, what did you decide about yourself in the context of your mother's love for you?

✍ JOURNAL ENTRY #98

For Journal Entries #89 through #97 (above), and their corresponding answers, look at your relationship with your wife or partner. Is she like your mother or opposite from your mother? Write "wife/partner same" or "wife/partner opposite" next to your answers above.

✍ JOURNAL ENTRY #99

If you are a father with a daughter, are you aware of the ramifications of your relating behavior in your relationship?

Motherly Influence #3: How your mother dealt with issues around money and its influence on you

How did your mom deal with money issues and how did this behavior influence your relationship with money? Your mother's relationship to money may also influence how you treat women with respect to money matters.

Whether or not your mother worked, how and if she contributed financially as well as her spending habits all play a role in your relationship with women when it comes to money. Maybe you had a mom who gave you money when you wanted to buy something and money wasn't a source of conflict. Maybe your mother was a stay-at-home mom or worked when you needed her around. Maybe your mom and dad fought about money, and your mom was devalued for her contribution around the home. Maybe your mom was a spender and your dad complained bitterly about it in front of you.

It's important to be aware of how these dynamics around money and work are playing out in your relationships now (especially if conflict is in the air).

✍ JOURNAL ENTRY #100

Did your mom stay at home? If so, do you consciously (or unconsciously) think your wife should stay at home, even if she wants to work?

✐ JOURNAL ENTRY #101

Is your wife absorbed in her work? If so, does it bring up the old pain of not getting enough attention when you were young or feeling lonely because your mom was home with you as a child?

✐ JOURNAL ENTRY #102

Do you fight about money because you saw your parents argue and it feels "normal"?

The intent of asking you to consider these questions is simply to raise your level of awareness around a topic that may have many limiting beliefs learned in your childhood. Without an awareness of these childhood influences, you may experience conflicting beliefs, chaos, and hurt that may result in divorce and bankruptcy. With this awareness, you may make better decisions with your partner (or future partner).

✐ JOURNAL ENTRY #103

What do you remember about your mother and saving/spending money?

✐ JOURNAL ENTRY #104

What beliefs and behaviors about saving and spending money did you adopt or reject?

✐ JOURNAL ENTRY #105

How is your wife (or partner) similar or different with respect to these topics?

✍ JOURNAL ENTRY #106

What do you remember about your mother regarding managing and investing money?

✍ JOURNAL ENTRY #107

What beliefs and behaviors about managing and investing money did you adopt or reject?

✍ JOURNAL ENTRY #108

How is your wife similar or different with respect to these topics?

✍ JOURNAL ENTRY #109

What was your mother's role in the family regarding money?

✍ JOURNAL ENTRY #110

Is your wife's role similar or different in your current relationship?

✍ JOURNAL ENTRY #111

Were the discussions your mother and father had around money peaceful or full of conflict?

✍ JOURNAL ENTRY #112

What position did your mom take?

✍ JOURNAL ENTRY #113

What position did your dad take?

 **JOURNAL ENTRY #114**

Is this dynamic present in your current or previous relationship(s) when it comes to matters of money?

CHAPTER 9

Honoring Your Father and Mother

Why is it important to honor your parents?

Forgiveness, While Challenging, Can Pay Off

When you explore the influences of your mother and father (or parental equivalents), you may find some experiences you resent, and those feelings are normal. Feel free to acknowledge any sad feelings you have about your past and your upbringing.

As part of Your Men's Journey to become a better man, it is important to avoid spending a lot of time resenting your parents and instead make the shift to honor them. Honoring your mother and father will help you embrace your life as *your own*. It will enable you to take full responsibility for your life going forward, free of blaming your parents for actions and events in the past that can't be changed. What *may* change is your future … and how it changes is *based on your future decisions*.

The following tips may help you honor your father and mother:

- **Acknowledge the good and bad traits.** Aspects of your father and mother live in you. The good and bad traits of your parents shaped who you are as a man. Pushing away these aspects of your parents means pushing away important parts of yourself.

- **Recognize the source of your positive traits.** Some of your parents' negative traits birthed your positive traits. For example, if your father (or father equivalent) wasn't emotionally available, you may have vowed never to cause your kids the pain you felt from *not* getting his attention. If your mom didn't nurture you with touch or words, the pain you felt from *not* getting these things from her may have resulted in giving positive feelings to *your* children and possibly your spouse. You may have transformed less-than-admirable traits that hurt you into ones that make you stronger. Your emotional growth and willingness to forge a new path gives you the birthright to pass these new, positive, and emotionally healthy traits to your sons and daughters.

- **Be accountable.** As a grown, emotionally mature man, take full responsibility for your actions and words, and their consequences—intended or not. The time for blaming your dad (and/or mom) for how they raised you and for your choices and actions stops now.

- **Be empathetic.** Your father also had a father, and his skill set as a man, husband, and father was related to his experience growing up with his father. Your mother had a mother, and her skill set as woman, wife, and mother was related to her experience as well. Stand in their shoes and recognize the troubles your parents experienced emotionally while raising you.

- **Forgive your parents.** This is often the hardest part. Holding on to anger and resentment will block your success in life and in relationships. Forgiveness allows you to let go and move forward. Your mom and dad (or parental equivalents) were human, and they loved you the best way they knew how. They gave you the best they had, even if their best wasn't very good at times. Their job of raising you is finished, and any leftover parenting needs to be done by *you*.

If you find it hard to forgive your parent(s), search for empathy for them. Imagine what it was like for them as kids, and recognize they did the best they could with what they received (and what was modeled for them).

Having empathy for your parents' limitations due to their own upbringing is one way you may let go and move on. Remember your parents were kids once, and they had experiences with their parents that inevitably shaped how they thought about themselves and their role as parents.

If you struggle to understand and forgive your parents because their behaviors may have been egregious, seek professional guidance. Some situations really do need the expertise of a professional, such as a trained family therapist who specializes in the leftover damage of family dynamics. Find the right person to help you and one with whom you connect.

Blaming your parent(s) for things beyond their control is pointless. Let your newfound awareness of *your* behaviors and their consequences be your guide. Your new awareness now blesses you with the opportunity to choose new choices: Behave in reaction to what happened during your childhood or behave based on your discoveries of this newfound awareness.

Any of the above tips may have significant and positive impacts on releasing yourself and your parents from events in the past. The ultimate way to honor your parents is to live your life honorably, learn from past mistakes, and make yourself and your parents proud of you as you go forward in life.

Is this the kind of man you want to be?

CHAPTER 10

Roadmap Step #4— Identify Blocks

What's in the way of you having what you want?

✓	Roadmap Step #1	Create Support for Yourself
✓	Roadmap Step #2	Speak Your Truth
✓	Roadmap Step #3	Declare Your Want
YOU ARE HERE	Roadmap Step #4	Identify Blocks
	Roadmap Step #5	Break Through Old Ways of Being
	Roadmap Step #6	Embody Responsibility
	Roadmap Step #7	Integrate and Manifest

Mike's Story (Part 4)

Mike had some homework to do before his next men's group session. Each man was to come prepared to talk about fatherly influences and share what he learned about the relationship with his father.

A more experienced man in the group, who was facilitating that night, suggested that Mike do his best to recall the aspects of his relationship with his dad (i.e., how his dad related to him):

- Did his dad display his feelings? If so, how?

- How did his dad treat his mom?

- How was his dad with money?

- How did his father demonstrate in his daily life the "what it meant to be a man" model?

The experienced man in the group explained that, by placing attention on the various aspects of his relationship with his father, each man would learn a lot about himself. He encouraged the men to stay open to the possibility of identifying some faulty beliefs and behaviors possibly handed down from their father. Awareness of these hidden beliefs and behaviors would allow each man to make an active declaration of a different belief and behavior that would serve him. This active declaration would be essential to each man's pursuit of making a big change in his life.

Mike recalled how his dad rarely seemed happy and was always working. Mike remembered how his dad wasn't very affectionate to him or to his mother, and didn't spend much one-on-one time with him. His dad seemed irritable a lot of the time.

As for money, Mike's dad seemed to provide the essentials and rarely had extra money for fun stuff. Mike struggled to recall seeing his dad buy things for himself. His mom and dad often got into disagreements around money. Still, Mike knew his dad loved him, even though they spent little time together.

Mike remembered that, more often than not, he heard his dad say, "I work so that you kids can have a good life."

However, not all of Mike's memories were negative. Mike thought about his father's good qualities. Mike's dad had a strong sense of community and often went out of his way to serve others less fortunate. He always talked about the importance of appreciating what one had versus focusing on what one didn't have. He had a strong work ethic that Mike still carried with him. Mike knew that, when the chips were down, his dad thought a man should get things done without complaining about it.

He used to say, "A man's gotta do what a man's gotta do."

According to his mother, Mike's dad used to be exciting and full of dreams, yet he never seemed interested in hearing about Mike's big ideas. According to what Mike's mother told him, when his dad and mom got married, baby Mike arrived quickly, and his dad had to get a real job. He put his dream of opening a restaurant on the back burner.

Maybe the reason Mike initially had a tough time answering the question about his "hot want" was because he never saw anyone—his dad in particular—"go for it" and go after what he really wanted. When Mike got big ideas, his father shut him down.

Mike pondered the similarities between his own behaviors and those of his father. Mike came to discover that his relationship with his father had shaped him as a man in several ways:

- Like his dad, Mike worked a lot and didn't do much for himself.

- When he was home, he was cranky.

- He made a lot of money but not a lot of friends.

- Initially, his marriage was exciting and intimate. Once the kids came along, things were never the same with his wife. Their relationship was more about the kids than about each other.

It slowly dawned on Mike that much of what he had observed growing up was occurring right now in his household, and he seemed to be the cause of it. While Mike strove *not* to be like his dad, in many ways he was *just like him.*

The larger question of "What does it mean to be a man?" stumped Mike. Yes, he provided food and shelter and loved his family but, in the areas around parenting and the relationship with his wife, Mike's only reference was his dad—and he was quickly coming to terms with the fact that he wanted a new way of living his life rather than his dad's way.

For Mike to have a chance of salvaging his marriage (or finding a successful, new one), he would have to make some big changes, and "what it meant to be a man" was going to play an important role. Mike was beginning to see a definite relationship between getting his "hot want" and being the man he was meant to be.

Useful Things to Know

Identifying the blocks that prevent you from having your "hot want" requires a multipronged approach to knowing yourself. More often than not, you—and no one else—are getting in your own way. Typically, there are learned behaviors and unconscious limiting beliefs operating in the background. While your mother influences you in different ways, your father influences you the most *when it comes to being a man.*

There are several common "inner" obstacles confronting most men in their pursuit of what it means to be a man. Being consciously aware of them is the first step; moving forward in pursuit of your "hot want" despite the obstacles is where your opportunity for growth lies.

- **Your history with your father may have only partially informed you.** Because you watched your father be a man in every sense of the word, your relationship with him has shaped your view of what a man is today … and what a man isn't. For example, how your father related to you, spoke, emoted, dressed, treated your mother, worked, relaxed, and parented all had an imprinting effect. You watched what worked and what didn't work for him. As you are probably experiencing now, what didn't work for your father is also not working for you.

- **You had no clear, effective male role model.** For you, there may have been no male role model in your home or in your life. Your father (or equivalent male figure) may have lacked the skills and know-how to parent well due to his own lack of a male role model.

  Most fathers of this generation—and several preceding ones—are off at work, leaving the day-to-day task of raising the boy(s) to the mother. This is in stark contrast to the agrarian society prevalent in previous centuries. In the agrarian society, it was typical to see the son out in the fields, interacting with his father, thus getting more male modeling.

  In addition, with women becoming more independent, and being more important work-force contributors since World War II, men are still at a loss in terms of how to interact in an effective, masculine way with women in the workplace.

  The impact of this societal shift is that many boys and men are searching for what it means to be a man in today's world. In the interim, they are functioning from an outdated model of what it means to be a man, using an incomplete reference that does not serve them in their relationships and lives.

- **You may have had addiction and abuse in your family.** Unfortunately, alcoholism, addictions, emotional abuse, and physical abuse from fathers were a way of life for many sons growing up. Many men carry the emotional wounds of their past into the present day, and the effects of these wounds are coupled with not having an ideal male role model. For these men, deep emotional healing is the only way to step into being the men they are meant to be.

  If you are one of these men, healing these deep emotional wounds will lead you to being able to define who you are as a man without shame.

- **You may have emulated antiquated role models.** While the images of John Wayne, the Marlboro Man, and high-profile sports figures are firmly imprinted in many male minds—ideas of what it "means to be a man in today's world"—these images are just that ... *images*. They all fall short in terms of real men an*d real* lives.

  The definition of what it means to be a man in today's world is up for grabs. In other words, you have a big say in defining what it means to be a man and deciding how you apply your own definition to your life.

- **You may be carrying limiting beliefs.** Maybe you carry unconscious limiting beliefs handed down from your dad and/ or resulting from your relationship (or lack thereof) with him.

  "Limiting beliefs" refer to the thoughts and/or stories you tell yourself that do not support you in living in your masculine power. These beliefs are often associated with events that happened to you when you were young. Often, when an emotionally injurious event happens, your still-forming young mind personalizes what happened, and you make unconscious conclusions about yourself.

For example, if you tried very hard to do a good job on a task for your dad, and then he yelled at and criticized you, you might have unconsciously decided, "I'm not good enough." With that conclusion, you programmed a behavior to prove the belief. Fast forward to your adult life, and a number of these beliefs and behaviors have been operating underneath the surface for quite some time.

Other examples of unconscious limiting beliefs are thoughts like "I'm not worthy" or "I'm not lovable." Transcending the beliefs that don't serve you as a man is one aspect of your inner men's work because limiting beliefs impact the choices you make and affect how you behave in any given situation. Until these limiting beliefs are uncovered, you may feel powerless to make any other choices because these beliefs limit your sense of reality.

Please note: There is a big difference between holding a limiting belief and using complaining, victim language. For example, when you say to yourself, "Nothing ever goes right for me," "I always have to work harder than everyone else," or "No one will ever really love me," you are expressing surface complaints and whiney, victim language. These words are not masculine and they are devoid of any power. Just try saying one of them and see how it feels.

Of course, other male adults may have contributed to your limiting beliefs, and your mother may have had an influence as well. Your task is to get familiar with the wide variety of imprinting that occurred in the context of your relationship with your dad or father figure. Being familiar with the traits, characteristics, wounds, and beliefs that don't serve you will give you the power of consciousness to make more positive decisions in the important areas of your life.

Action Steps for Identifying Blocks

This Roadmap step is about:

- Identifying what's getting in the way of being able to create what you want most in your life (your "hot want"); and

- Understanding how your ability to make the big change in your life relates to being the man you are meant to be.

As with anything that appears to be in your way, there are obvious and easy-to-identify external obstacles, such as a lack of knowledge, money, and time as well as a job and responsibilities. In addition, hidden internal obstacles often hold you back. Put more simply, *you are in your own way*. On your journey to becoming the man you want to be, it is imperative to claim your history fully.

Hopefully, the questions (and your answers) in Chapter 7, "Your Father," and Chapter 8, "Your Mother," helped guide you towards identifying your blocks and limiting beliefs. This is largely an assignment of awareness and, by reading these chapters and doing the exercises, you learned a lot about yourself as a man and got some powerful insights.

If this felt like a lot to do, it was. Wanting different results requires doing something different. Notice any resistance and avoid telling stories, such as "I don't have time," "This is stupid," or "My family was perfect." If you can focus, commit, and go into action, I *promise* that good things will come out of this.

After you review your answers to the questions in Chapter 7, here are some new questions to ponder:

JOURNAL ENTRY #115

Do (or did) any of the beliefs and behaviors you discovered contribute to your wake-up call? If so, how? What were the consequences to you? What were the consequences to others?

 JOURNAL ENTRY #116

Are any old beliefs or behaviors (unrelated to money) from your dad getting in the way of you having your "hot want"? If yes, create a list called "Blocks" and write down whatever you discover.

 JOURNAL ENTRY #117

Identify the area with which you are struggling about money (e.g., self-worth, spending, saving, earning, or investing) and see if any old beliefs or behaviors show up and get in the way of you having your "hot want." If yes, add to your list of "Blocks" and write down whatever you discover.

 JOURNAL ENTRY #118

Have your struggles with money contributed to your wake-up call? If so, how? What were the consequences to you? What were the consequences to others?

Sometimes the absence of power is all that is in the way of manifesting your "hot want." Your answers to the questions in Chapter 8, "Your Mother," may invariably point to a lack of power and/or old beliefs and behaviors that you now exhibit around women (resulting from your experience with your mother when you were growing up). The emotional wounding you may have experienced with your mother may have created certain unhealthy, chaotic, and sabotaging behaviors with women. It might have even contributed to your wake-up call.

Now that you have done the work in Chapter 8, review your answers in each section and answer these questions:

 JOURNAL ENTRY #119

Is your power available to you? Is the lack of power preventing you from moving forward in your life? If your block is around the lack of power, add it to your list of "Blocks."

JOURNAL ENTRY #120

Do (or did) these beliefs and behaviors contribute to your wake-up call? If so, how? What were the consequences to you? What were the consequences to others?

JOURNAL ENTRY #121

Are any old beliefs or behaviors from your mom getting in the way of you having your "hot want"? If yes, add them to your list of "Blocks." At this juncture, it is important to make the connection between these behaviors and your wake-up call, see how they contributed to your wake-up call, and understand how your lack of power may be interfering with accomplishing what you have set out to do (i.e., your "hot want").

JOURNAL ENTRY #122

With insight on your past beliefs and behaviors, what are some new, positive beliefs and behaviors that you can articulate for yourself to help you attain your "hot want"?

Worthwhile Wins on Which to Set Your Sights

- You will know your father from a new place.

- You will be able to honor your father.

- You will know your mother from a new place.

- You will be able to honor your mother.

- Your will positively challenge your own fatherhood.

- You will learn more about the parts of yourself that were out of view.

- You will have more awareness of why you have been doing what you have been doing.

- With this awareness of your "whys," you will be able to make new choices, which may lead to new results in your life.

- You will have a working definition of what it means to be a man according to *you*.

- You will have successfully accessed your masculine power to serve you in attaining your "hot want."

CHAPTER 11

Roadmap Step #5—Break Through Old Ways of Being

*How do you get unstuck and
move past what's blocking you?*

✓	Roadmap Step #1	Create Support for Yourself
✓	Roadmap Step #2	Speak Your Truth
✓	Roadmap Step #3	Declare Your Want
✓	Roadmap Step #4	Identify Blocks
YOU ARE HERE	Roadmap Step #5	Break Through Old Ways of Being
	Roadmap Step #6	Embody Responsibility
	Roadmap Step #7	Integrate and Manifest

Mike's Story (Part 5)

Mike had to do some personal work—*men's work*—by examining and confronting his actions, his limiting beliefs, and his childhood wounds, and coming to terms with their resulting consequences in his adult life. Put in simpler terms, it was time for him to emotionally grow up, take full responsibility for his life, and not blame others or stay stuck in unproductive patterns.

Mike felt the heaviness of what seemed to be the only two choices before him. He could do nothing, make no changes, and end up divorced and alone like his dad, or take a risk to open up, trust other people, and make some changes that might jeopardize his business and upset the financial apple cart with his wife (in which case, she might leave anyway).

Having done the exercises around the fatherly influences (see Chapter 7, "Your Father"), Mike felt a strange combination of surprise, astonishment, sadness, anger, and a little shame. He learned that, like his father, his belief about what it meant to be a good husband simply involved bringing home the bacon—and not much more.

He learned that he often put himself last. This created self-resentment that he then blamed on his wife. His tank was running empty. No wonder sex—or even the idea of it—left him feeling turned off and unmotivated. This also explained why he didn't feel like playing with his kids.

Mike learned that his distrust of men came from his relationship with his dad, who often let him down and made promises he broke. His dad wasn't available for him, so Mike became self-reliant to a fault. Mike learned to keep his distance from most men because he didn't have a close relationship with his dad and he honestly didn't know how to be close with men, let alone rely on them when it counted. This was most evident at his company, where all of his employees were men.

Mike's lack of trust explained why he took on so much of the workload and responsibility.

As Mike learned more about his father's upbringing, he imagined what his dad's life must have been like growing up. Mike felt empathy for his father, which allowed him to forgive his father for his shortcomings and transgressions. The key for Mike was to make room for what was possible by simply noticing, forgiving, and letting go.

The opportunity that lay before Mike was immense. He thought about the positive opposite of his current shortcomings (as they related to his upbringing); however, instead of getting discouraged, he decided to look at what was *possible*.

Mike saw the possibility of saving his marriage and being more involved in his kid's day-to-day lives. He pictured that, if he could learn to trust the men at his company, he might find more balance with his work and home life. He saw that, if he built some quality male friendships—not simply friendships for watching football and having a few beers—he might get the kind of male camaraderie he'd always wanted.

To do this, Mike knew he had to learn to include *his needs* more often. He would have to learn to trust other men if he were going to let go of some control and gain quality time in his life for himself and his family. Mike would need to experience and show his feelings by embracing his vulnerability as a sign of strength.

It struck him that, if he did this work, he would become a *model* for his two boys and ensure they didn't repeat the pain of his mistakes. He would also bring a more mature representation of a man to his daughter, so her frame of reference would be more positive. This made Mike feel proud.

These changes would be no small task and would require every ounce of determination, courage, patience, and resolve Mike had. He knew he would need an identifiable outcome to be accountable to his strategy and to move forward. He needed inner strength—his Wildman—to assist him. For those who don't recognize this term, it comes from Robert Bly's book, *Iron John* (Addison-Wesley, 1990). The Wildman is a character filled with vitality, representing a masculine energy source available to all men.

Mike was ready to take responsibility for his life as a man in a new way. He knew that going into action might be messy and he might screw up, yet he was willing to risk going after what he wanted. Not going after what he wanted no longer felt like a choice. He would simply have to man up and step up … and deal with the consequences.

Useful Things to Know

It may come as no surprise that, as a man, you spend a lot of time thinking "in your head"; however, there is a whole world of feelings, instincts, power, and intuition living in your body. No matter how rational you think you are, it can be very useful to tap into the Wildman inside when you need energy, courage, and commitment to confront life's changes.

When you have spent a long time acting unconsciously on beliefs that no longer serve you, you need every ounce of strength and resolve to reprogram your old way of being. How do you know when you've tapped your inner strength, your Wildman, and your masculine power? You will feel it and you will believe you can do anything you set out to do—a feeling of vitality.

When a man has access to his full masculine power, he charges forward into action. He takes risks and accepts full responsibility. If or when he makes mistakes, he acknowledges they happened, searches for the lesson, and keeps pressing towards his goal.

Once you have identified what's in your way of having what you want in your life (i.e., your old beliefs and behaviors), it's time to move into action and break through the old ways if you want different results. As the old Nike slogan said, "Just *do* it."

Remember: Inside you is a gut instinct and a heart that drive you. Remember, your head is a useful tool; however, the *real* action is in your body where your feelings and energy source reside.

Step out of your comfort zone, take a risk, and trust the strength of your intuition.

Action Steps for Breaking through Old Ways of Being

When my former business partner and I conducted men's retreats, we combined the Roadmap steps from this book with physical exercise, so men would get out of their heads and into their bodies (where their feelings and their Wildman reside). The idea was to advance their mental and emotional learning before, during, and after their physical exercise.

Any kind of physical exercise worked as long as we coupled it with reflection. You can use this technique any way you want. You can mountain climb, bike, hike, walk, do yoga, cross-country ski, swim, or even play golf. The idea is to use the physical activity to support your breakthrough by getting in your body.

Action Step: Review the nonserving beliefs and behaviors in your journal entries from Chapter 10

✍ JOURNAL ENTRY #123

On a fresh piece of paper, draw a line down the middle from top to bottom. On the left side of the page, write the nonserving beliefs and behaviors. You may have one or many nonserving beliefs. List all of them because this is largely an exercise of awareness. Look at your list, and simply notice and be aware of the beliefs and behaviors that have been operating inside you. With the ones that don't serve you, notice the impact to yourself and others.

What would it be like to not have these beliefs/behaviors run your life anymore? How would your life be different and/or better? Notice how these nonserving beliefs make you feel when you contemplate the consequences of not changing them.

Remember: Your ability as a man to create these unintended consequences from your unconscious beliefs and behaviors is *nothing* compared to your power and ability to create new consequences from consciously formed beliefs and behaviors.

Action Step: Turn your nonserving beliefs into positive beliefs and behaviors to attain your "hot want"

✍🏻 JOURNAL ENTRY #124

Looking at your nonserving beliefs and behaviors on the left side of the page, contemplate and write down on the right hand side of paper positive opposite beliefs and behaviors of each of them.

Action Step: Envision life consequences that may occur as a result of your new beliefs and behaviors

---

✍🏻 JOURNAL ENTRY #125

Referring to Journal Entry #124, ask yourself these questions and write down the answers for each new positive belief/behavior: What kind of positive consequences would occur if you acted on them? What kind of positive things would happen to you? What kind of positive things would happen to those around you?

Action Step: Consider what kind of man you would need to be to act on these beliefs and behaviors

Here's a hint: In Mike's case, he would have to be a trusting man, who would be willing to be vulnerable with his feelings and practice self-love in order to be able to love others. This is a good time to align with your core values and commit to pursuing your "hot want."

🖎 JOURNAL ENTRY #126

Create an affirmation statement about yourself as a man and write it down. For example, if your "hot want" relates to your relationships, your affirmation statement might be, "I am a man of integrity and honor, committed to bringing my heart, power, and masculinity into my relationships."

Action Step: Craft a specific and measurable outcome you would like to see and believe you will achieve

Once you have crafted this statement at a contextual level, it's time to be specific about with whom, when, where, and how. The idea here is to pick something that is doable and in an area of relevance to what's important and in alignment with your affirmation statement. It's advisable to start with a small, relevant outcome that you can actually accomplish.

🖎 JOURNAL ENTRY #127

Looking at your newly crafted affirmation statement in Journal Entry #126, with the intent that it aids you in manifesting your "hot want," envision an action that moves you in the right direction. It needs to be specific, measurable, attainable, relevant, and time bound. A 12-year-old should be able to ask, "Did you do this?"

Action Step: Ask for support

Do you have a trusted male friend? Do you belong to a men's group? Do you have a coach or therapist? What person in your life might you ask to hold you accountable (in addition to yourself)? Asking someone to hold you accountable may make a big difference in manifesting your "hot want."

Additionally and optionally, now would be a good time for those who have a spiritual practice to ask for courage, support, and perseverance from your spiritual source so you may break through.

Action Step: Perform some kind of physical action to seal your commitment to your outcome and then let go

Here are some suggestions:

- Have with you a list of the nonserving beliefs and behaviors of which you want to let go, and then write down your "hot want" statement from Chapter 6, "Roadmap Step #3—Declare Your Want," Journal Entry #11).

- Read it, review it, and envision it.

- Review your affirmation statement from "Action Step: Consider what kind of man you would need to be to act on these beliefs and behaviors" (Journal Entry #126). Close your eyes and see yourself as the kind of man you will need to be. Envision yourself with those qualities, doing the types of things a man like that does.

- With this attitude in your body, begin a physical activity.

- At the halfway point in your ritual, stop what you're doing and dispose of the old beliefs and behaviors. You might say, "I hereby release these old beliefs and behaviors as they no longer serve me." You might rip up a piece of paper with your old beliefs on it, or you might scream at the top of your lungs, "I am done with all of that!" Do whatever has meaning for you.

- Review the positive opposite beliefs and behaviors to see the positive outcomes for you and your loved ones. Say them aloud or to yourself.

- Restart your physical activity.

Worthwhile Wins on Which to Set Your Sights

- You will get a new awareness of operating beliefs and behaviors that don't serve you.

- You will gain the ability to make different positive choices about yourself and engage in different behaviors to support your attainment of your "hot want."

- You will envision new possibilities and positive life consequences as a result of having new beliefs.

- You will gain more courage, momentum, and confidence with each successive action step.

- You will access internal courage and strength to support you as you go into action.

- You will feel it's OK to make a mistake, knowing you will learn more towards achieving your "hot want."

- You will have the ability to tap into an internal masculine power that may not have been accessible to you before.

CHAPTER 12

Roadmap Step # 6— Embody Responsibility

How do you move forward responsibly?

	Roadmap Step #1	Create Support for Yourself
✓	Roadmap Step #1	Create Support for Yourself
✓	Roadmap Step #2	Speak Your Truth
✓	Roadmap Step #3	Declare Your Want
✓	Roadmap Step #4	Identify Blocks
✓	Roadmap Step #5	Break Through Old Ways of Being
YOU ARE HERE	Roadmap Step #6	Embody Responsibility
	Roadmap Step #7	Integrate and Manifest

Mike's Story (Part 6)

Mike had learned a lot about himself over the last month, and he could already feel the difference. After focusing on breaking through and getting unstuck, Mike decided his next step was to take the bull by the horns and sign up for a men's weekend workshop about understanding women to help him relate better to his wife. Lastly, Mike dusted off his bike and, after much review of his recent insights, set an intention to go for a ride to "pedal out" all the old beliefs and behaviors.

When Mike arrived at the top of the mountain, he got off his bike and performed a ceremony to release his old behaviors. He closed his eyes and envisioned himself as the type of man he wanted to be. He imagined himself embodying the positive beliefs and behaviors that would show he was a better man in his marriage and a better father to his kids.

He committed to allowing his core values to guide him. He vowed to bring his masculinity, power, and heart into his relationships as much as possible. With his "hot want" statement memorized and emblazoned in his mind, he pedaled back to his new life that lay ahead of him, full of confidence.

Mike knew he would need rock-solid confidence to move forward responsibly. Those closest to him would probably expect his old behaviors to show up. Mike would have to be impeccable with his words, actions, and choices, and take full responsibility for their consequences—intended or not.

Mike knew he might end up having a few conversations with people close to him, and would have to own his past behaviors and their impact. He was dreading this in one way; in another way, he felt energized, knowing these conversations would help him move forward with integrity.

Thinking back, Mike felt badly about some of his actions and the way he treated his wife. He was holding on to grudges about some things she said and did. For example, one time he came home very excited about a new business direction, and she shot him down, not even willing to listen. Then, there was a time when his old buddies came into town with concert tickets, and she gave him hell for wanting to go; a year later, he was still mad about it. Forgiveness didn't come easily for Mike, and he knew forgiving himself and his wife was the only way forward.

Useful Things to Know

We men tend to wake up later in life. When you do become conscious, you are aware of your past unconsciousness and your corresponding behaviors—as well as the consequences—especially on others. A conscious man takes responsibility for these consequences, and sets an intention to clean up any situations he can and allow himself to go forward cleanly.

This is not work for the faint of heart. Breaking through old beliefs and behaviors might be challenging mentally, physically, emotionally, and spiritually. Acknowledging the damage you've done might be fiercely painful.

Still, as you resolve to stay awake, your masculine core values will play a huge role in how you move forward in life. Your personal integrity will become primary. Your accountability will be a cornerstone of your choices, actions, and words. Most importantly, your ability to forgive—first yourself and then others—will be something on which you will need to work actively if you want to keep moving forward.

You might feel horrible about some of your past actions towards others; however, without forgiving yourself for what has happened, you are avoiding taking full responsibility. Forgiveness is often the first step in taking responsibility for your actions.

Action Steps for Embodying Responsibility

Will you forgive yourself? Will you take full responsibility for your actions and words? The work in this next Action Step is sometimes the hardest for men. Take it seriously and slowly, and know this next step is one of the most important in your personal transformation.

Action Step: Forgive another person or yourself

Forgiveness doesn't have to be hard or take a long time. It doesn't mean that what happened in the past is acceptable. I invite you to consider the possibility that you may release yourself (and others) from feelings of anger, shame, and resentment that keep you tied to the past.

✍ JOURNAL ENTRY #127

Consider applying these steps when working on forgiveness, and answer these questions: Are you holding yourself personally responsible for your words, choices, or actions that have caused somebody else pain? Are you holding somebody else personally responsible for the words, choices, or actions that have caused you pain? Are you holding a grudge? Is your inability to forgive yourself or others holding you back in life and in your relationships?"

If you answered "yes" to any of the above questions, now answer these questions: If you are holding yourself responsible, what feelings arise inside of you? Do you feel mad at yourself? Do you feel ashamed? What is the underlying truth about your feelings of shame and/or anger? Are you experiencing sadness, fear, or loss/grief? If you are holding someone else responsible, what feeling(s) do you have towards this person? Do you feel angry? What's true about your anger towards this person? Are you experiencing sadness, fear, or loss/grief?

Explore your feelings a little more deeply and see if you can get underneath the reactionary feelings of anger or shame. We all share fundamental core emotions. When you are interested in what's *more* true about your shame and/or anger, you may free yourself from the grip of resentment and the temporary inability to forgive.

Avoiding forgiveness of yourself or others may feel righteous and powerful at times. That behavior might be a harmful choice and a reaction designed to protect you from experiencing your deep emotions. In the long run, this failure to connect to those deep places inside yourself in order to forgive yourself—or somebody else—may block the success of your relationships.

Action Step: Ask yourself what or who really matters

The next step is something you might not expect: Decide what or who really matters to you. Who or what do you really care about? Maybe you care about young children. Maybe you care about your wife, kids, best friend, animals, your fellow man, your parents, the planet, or even your garden. Maybe you care about telling the truth. Maybe you care about your own values.

Connect to the part of you that knows how to care, and let it fill your chest. Let yourself feel how much you actually care. Disengage from your reactive and toxic anger, and reengage with a different kind of energy (i.e., your caring energy).

Action Step: Consider the other person

With caring feeling in your body, consider the idea that the person who hurt you *also* cares about something deeply, and was most likely reacting to some pain they felt, in survival mode and unconscious about how their actions affected you and others.

The sad fact is that *hurt people hurt others*. Even if you feel as if someone were indeed "out to get you," remember the possibility that the other person was hurt by someone else in the past, and may think "dogging you" is the only way to get their needs met.

Consider the fact that many people are victims themselves and are capable of becoming unconscious perpetrators. This doesn't excuse their behavior, but it does make it seem less personal.

Action Step: Find empathy for the other person and yourself

This next step may take a leap of faith. Take a deep breath, find empathy for the other person, and see their humanness. Acknowledge that this person has their own patterns and history with which to deal, and is on his or her own path.

Wish that person well. Visualize the same thing for yourself if *you* hurt someone. Remember your own patterns and history and your own path. Wish *yourself* well.

When embarking on forgiveness, you are forgiving *the person*, not the act. It is healthy to have standards and expectations for your behavior, and the act is completed. Holding someone accountable for something in the past is futile, and it works against the process of forgiveness.

At the same time, it's important to make sure you protect yourself against any person who may have a pattern of harming you emotionally. Keep your distance, if need be, and establish clear boundaries to keep yourself safe.

Action Step: Take responsibility for your choices, words, and actions, and move into action

You may have an ex-wife or former business partner, who was at the receiving end of your less-than-stellar behavior., or maybe it's a relationship with an old girlfriend or an old guy friend that ended poorly because of your previous inability to take responsibility. You might have grown or even young children with whom you may share what you know now about your actions, words, and choices.

In the Twelve-Step program for Alcoholics Anonymous, the ninth step states, "Made direct amends to such people wherever possible, except when to do so would injure them or others." Part of being a man who steps up and takes responsibility for his actions, words, and choices includes this very important step.

When you are up for it—whoever "they" are—ask their permission to share your awareness of the impact of your actions, words, and choices and acknowledge how they affected, hurt, or dishonored this person. You can suggest writing a letter or having a face-to-face meeting.

Consider this process flow in your communication:

- Be clear on your wrongdoing.

- Detach from any outcome you imagine might happen or want to see happen.

- Acknowledge the action, inaction, words, and choices you did and admit all of them.

- Consider the consequences to them emotionally, physically, spiritually, mentally, and financially, and empathically consider how you might feel if these things were done to you.

- Empathically share those feelings in such a way that the other person understands you are relatively aware of the hurt you caused. Be sure to include an apology. It might look something like this: "I imagine if these things happened to me, I would be angry, afraid, betrayed, and/or distrustful." You might ask them, if you are face to face, to share their feelings, in which case you need to share back to them what you heard so they feel heard. Then you may say, "I am truly sorry for my actions and how it has made you feel." Be sure to acknowledge the feelings.

- Offer a gesture to get back into the right relationship with this person—only if this person is open to being back in a relationship with you and it is healthy for you to be in a relationship with them. You might consider offering some gesture of accountability on your part to begin to make things right. They may refuse. The point is for them to understand that your gesture is symbolic of your intent to make things right again. It's extremely important that your actions become congruent with your words.

When you speak from integrity and accountability, the act of going to them and taking responsibility for your words, choices, and actions send clear messages. These actions say, "You are someone who matters to me in my life, and I care enough to make it right."

It is never too late to take responsibility for old behavior. Regardless of whether they are receptive, you are taking responsibility to restore your own integrity. You are doing this for you. Embodying responsibility is important enough … *to you.*

Action Step: Stay awake

After you have become conscious of your hurtful behaviors, the only way to avoid these same behaviors is to commit to being on a personal path to know yourself better, and consistently seek the support of others who are on their own path and who resonate with you.

Find men who you give you feedback and ask you good questions. Chapter 5, "Roadmap Step #2—Speak Your Truth," suggest that joining or creating a men's group is foundational to succeed in staying awake.

You will help them (and they will help you) stay awake. Your Men's Journey is a multifaceted trip. Waking up means *getting awake* and *staying awake,* so you may do your personal work.

Wake up!

Worthwhile Wins on Which to Set Your Sights

- You will find people trust you more as your words and actions align.

- Your relationships may start to heal.

- Your relationships may start to thrive.

- You might feel better about yourself.

- You might set a good example for your children.

- You might live a more conscious masculine life.

- You may develop integrity with yourself.

CHAPTER 13

Roadmap Step #7—Integrate and Manifest

How do you integrate this Roadmap process into other areas of your life?

✓	Roadmap Step #1	Create Support for Yourself
✓	Roadmap Step #2	Speak Your Truth
✓	Roadmap Step #3	Declare Your Want
✓	Roadmap Step #4	Identify Blocks
✓	Roadmap Step #5	Break Through Old Ways of Being
✓	Roadmap Step #6	Embody Responsibility
YOU ARE HERE	Roadmap Step #7	Integrate and Manifest

What You've Already Accomplished

You've taken some major steps in Your Men's Journey to become a conscious man. You've learned what to do in order to answer your wake-up call with as much personal power as possible. You've learned how to grow up and step up.

Specifically, your new skills include:

- Getting and knowing what support is, understanding why it's important, and knowing where you might find it

- Accessing your truth, speaking it to others, and learning from others who are on this journey beside you

- Identifying your masculine core values

- Identifying your "hot want"

- Identifying what's in the way of having what you want

- Learning about your father's influence

- Learning about your mother's influence

- Honoring your mother and father

- Breaking through where you're stuck

- Forgiving yourself and others

- Taking responsibility for the consequences of your actions and acting with integrity

Roadmap Step #7 is an invitation to pull together what you've learned, take a deeper and more focused dive into the areas of your life that need your attention, and manifest outcomes based on your choices. At this point, you have the option of choosing where you want to focus first and taking the headlong plunge into the area that calls to you.

Choosing from the Menu

Congratulations are in order for your efforts thus far! You have accomplished most of the hardest work Your Men's Journey requires after you have completed the previous action steps. Next is the opportunity to take everything you have learned into your everyday life and turn it up several notches in the area most important to you.

The next six chapters of this book focus on these topics:

- "The Good Father" (Chapter 14)

- "The Good Partner/Husband" (Chapter 15)

- "The Masculine Leader" (Chapter 16)

- "Real Male Friendships" (Chapter 17)

- "Navigating a Conscious Divorce" (Chapter 18)

- "The Next Man" (Chapter 19)

Each focus chapter offers things to think about, questions to ponder and answer, and a personal growth plan to complete (if the chapter warrants it). You may go through the chapters sequentially, or pick the ones that apply to the areas in your life where you want to grow.

These chapters will help you solidify how you want to move forward in the areas most important to you. You might spend the rest of your life improving yourself in these areas. Remember: This work is more of a marathon than a sprinting race.

Commit to staying awake and following your path. Now that you are in motion, stay in motion. Staying awake lets you leverage the momentum you have established to improve the ongoing quality of your life as a man.

The Roadmap sequence is now a tool in your arsenal. You may use it whenever you hit a speed bump in Your Men's Journey. You may use the process as a checklist for action whenever things get tough.

With the next chapter in sight, answer these questions:

- Do you have support right now? What support do you need? (Roadmap Step #1)

- Are you speaking your truth? (Roadmap Step #2)

- Do you know what you want? Have you declared it? (Roadmap Step #3)

- What's in your way? (Roadmap Step # 4)

- How much of your being stuck relates to your old beliefs and patterns that you want to change? (Roadmap Step # 5)

- How might you take responsibility for your words, choices, and actions? What concrete actions might you choose to take to make this happen? (Roadmap Step #6)

Again, the Roadmap sequence is now a tool in your toolkit and you may use it as often as you become aware of the need.

From Integration to Manifestation

Now it's time to decide which chapter resonates most closely with the potential win you identified and your "hot want" statement.

Here are some tips for the next part of Your Men's Journey:

- **Be patient and as present as possible** to what is going on inside you, around you, and with other people. Remember: This is a journey, not a destination.

- **Spend time creating your growth plan.** What you put in, you get out.

- **Maintain support at all times,** whether with your male friends, your men's group, your therapist, your spouse, and/or your higher power. Ask for the kind of support you need (e.g., accountability, reminders, or physical assistance).

- **Move into action!** Notice what comes up as you take action. You may find it to be a good idea to hire a coach or form a men's We group (a three-man group with similar goals in mutual support of each other). (For more information, see "My Programs" in the Resources section.)

- **Celebrate your wins.** When you celebrate the smallest wins, the bigger wins will come. If you acknowledge the small stuff, you acknowledge your progress and build momentum towards bigger wins coming your way. Many men feel challenged around receiving what they desire. Consider celebrating and expressing gratitude as practice when you reach small wins, especially if you have difficulty receiving.

- **Have fun!** Be attentive and respectful of yourself, and remember that this is supposed to make your life better. Have fun and laugh as you come to realizations about yourself.

- **This is a journey.** Pick the chapter on which you are going to focus. Focus on the man you want to be, and remember that it is a day-by-day, moment-by-moment process always happening in the present moment—the *now*. Whatever chapter you choose, be present day to day and moment to moment. Use your journal to track your days. When you have arrived at a satisfactory level, simply turn your attention to another chapter.

CHAPTER 14

The Good Father

What are the pillars of being the father your children need you to be?

A Perspective to Consider

Ask 10 people what they think a good father is, and you will probably get 10 different answers with some similarities. Ask those same people what they *desired most* from their father, and you may see a strong connection between what they desired and how they now define a good father.

You base parenting on what you desired the most. For example, if your father avoided affection with words and/or touch, and you wanted more affection, chances are you "know exactly what to do" to show affection to your kids because it is what you desired the most. This is true in many areas of parenting; I know this is true for my kids and me.

There is no right or wrong way to be a father; however, there are pillars of good, conscious fathering. How you put these elements together is up to you. I offer what I learned on my path of becoming a better father and a better man, and you might use the ideas here to design your own style of conscious fathering. The emphasis is on the word "conscious," meaning that you will have the opportunity to put together your own plan for developing yourself as a father.

At the end of this chapter, the Good Father Growth Plan gives you the opportunity to craft a plan in areas on which you wish to concentrate and put action into improving. *This is the shift from integration to manifestation.* Once you have integrated these new concepts into your way of thinking and awareness, you may then set out to manifest these concepts into your own reality by your design. You might use it as a written "game plan" that you may decide to execute.

As you put this plan together, you have an important duty. Being a man in the 21st century is a great responsibility with respect to teaching your sons and daughters about men.

You might focus on:

- Your financial freedom

- Principles of accountability and responsibility

- Improving your emotional literacy

- Adopting a mission of service in which to improve the world

Why do we men desire to do these things? Because kids are watching, communities need it, and the world might be a better place as a result.

Pillars of Good, Conscious Fathering

Here are some pillars of good, conscious fathering that you may discover useful to design your own style of fathering and to go to the next level.

Relational Presence

What is relational presence? "Presence" is the notion of "being here" and "relational" is the notion of "being with," so "relational presence" is the idea that, when you are with your kids, you are consciously awake and consciously present with them. Being in the moment with your children is the greatest gift you may give them. You might consider the gift of time as your present to them. Put another way, relational presence can be thought of as "Be here now … with the person in front of you."

As a father, I hope you understand and appreciate the impact of your physical and emotional presence on your children. Kids often say, "He spends time with me," when asked what they appreciate the most about their dad. Being with kids is central and valuable to them. You may *simply look at* your kids with your powerful "father eyes," and see them with love and approval.

If or when you are a father, you have an opportunity and a responsibility to relate to your sons and daughters mindfully. Your ability to create a safe container, your ability to listen, and your willingness to look at them with eyes that say, "I love you. I am proud of you. You can do anything you put your mind to doing," might go a long way in forming your child's positive self-image—an image they carry with them for the rest of their lives. Their self-images begin with you … so treat them right!

Relational presence requires you to listen for and see your children's positive qualities, which makes you a magnet for their best and naturally evokes *your* best.

Take your time to consider the following questions, and notice what goes on in your body. There is no right or wrong answer. Recall your answers from Chapter 7, "Your Father" (Journal Entries #12 through #76), and note where you are similar and dissimilar from your dad.

 **JOURNAL ENTRY #128**

How do you like to spend time with your kids?

 **JOURNAL ENTRY #129**

Do any of your father's traits show up in you when you are with your kids?

 **JOURNAL ENTRY #130**

What kind of attention did you want most from your father?

 **JOURNAL ENTRY #131**

How is your experience with your kids like and unlike your experience with your father?

Your answer(s) may lend insight on how to be with your kids.

Next, ask your kids *for their perspective* on what they love about being with you and listen to their feedback.

 **JOURNAL ENTRY #132**

What are you hearing from your kids? Look for the common theme with them.

 **JOURNAL ENTRY #133**

Are there areas you desire to focus more on?

 **JOURNAL ENTRY #134**

Are there areas to consider focusing less on?

Keep your answers in mind for your Good Father Growth Plan.

Relationship Modeling

Your role as a father includes being aware of the influence you have on your children when you interact with your partner, spouse, or ex-spouse—in other words, how you treat women. It means being responsible for your interactions as well as being accountable for them. Your daily interactions with the woman in your life show your kids, "This is how you treat a woman. This is how you talk to a woman. This is how you relate to a woman."

Living and relating from your masculine core values are important. In Chapter 3, "Starting Your Journey," we discussed masculine core male values (vitality, authenticity, honor, integrity, and accountability) and other core values by which you live.

Whatever values you live by, demonstrating them daily becomes a nonverbal "how to" model for your sons and daughters to emulate. Your modeling includes how you listen, communicate, care for the woman in your life, and respect and honor her. It also includes communicating your truth to her, even though she might disagree.

Take your time, consider the following questions, and notice what goes on in your body. There is no right or wrong answer.

- Do you recall if the masculine core value of vitality was present while watching your father?

- Do you demonstrate balanced vitality in your interactions with your partner or spouse?

- When you interact with your partner or spouse, are you in a strong, grounded state?

- Is your level of energy in check and modulated or do you over-whelm your spouse?

- Did your father honor your mother? If so, how?

- How do you honor your partner/spouse?

- Was your father's authenticity apparent in his interactions with your mom?

- How do you model authenticity with your kids?

- Regarding your father's integrity, was he in alignment with his words and actions when it came to interacting with your mom?

- Are your words and actions totally, often, or rarely aligned?

- Where might you improve?

- If you have boys, how do they interact with their mother?

- Is it similar to how you interact with their mother?

- What do you see?

- Did your father model accountability in his life or did he routinely blame others?

✍ JOURNAL ENTRY #135

Take notice of your answers to these questions and journal them when appropriate), and consider them when constructing your Good Father Growth Plan.

Male Role Modeling

Your father and other influential men in your life shaped your understanding of what it means to be a man, a leader, a friend, and a father. They provided you with a model for how to "be with men." You have the same influence on your boys. Your new responsibility is to evolve *past* your father's shortcomings (or that of another influential male figure in your life) and develop new strengths to pass down to your son.

The best way to do this is to live and embody your masculine core values in all you do by being aware of how your behavior shapes your son's definition of what a man is. Your sons are watching you, and they naturally want to emulate you.

Take your time, consider the following questions, and notice what goes on in your body. Use your responses to "Discovering Your Masculine Core Values Exercise" (Chapter 3, "Starting Your Journey") to support you in answering the following questions.

✍ JOURNAL ENTRY #136

Which of your masculine core values are present (and which ones are missing) in each of the following areas:

- Finances?
- Issues relating to women (including your daughter)?
- Issues relating to other men?
- Parenting?

Relationship with Your Daughter

Even if you have a young daughter, who is nowhere near marrying age, I want you to imagine that today is your daughter's wedding. Imagine seeing a young man (her husband-to-be) and knowing you may be spending weekends, holidays, and Sunday dinners with this young man.

Consider this: You play a significant role regarding the kind of man she will choose because, when your daughter gets older and becomes interested in boys, her frame of reference for men will be *you*!

I share this thought so you might be mindful of the influence you have on your daughter. Your simple, day-to-day relationship with her may show up in her life in various ways. Your unspoken power as "her first man" may affect the way she selects, interacts, and deals with men later in her life. Your ability to affirm, support, teach, and love her may affect her life as she grows up and have a lasting effect on her as an adult.

Take your time, consider the following questions, and notice what goes on in your body. There is no right or wrong answer.

✍ JOURNAL ENTRY #137

How do you currently relate to your daughter? Are any of the ways you relate to her similar to how you relate to your wife? How do your actions teach your daughter to behave? How do you spend time with your daughter? Based on your answers, are there any changes you desire to make?

Consider your answers when constructing your Good Father Growth Plan.

Accountability

Responsibility and accountability go hand in hand. "Responsibility" means having duties or tasks you must complete. "Accountability" means having to accept the results of your tasks as well as the consequences of your choices, words, and actions.

The best way to demonstrate responsibility and accountability in your fathering is to:

- Live your truth and model it in all you do and say.

- Create agreements around responsibilities with your kids (e.g., household chores) and create clarity for accountability. Be sure to agree on and verbalize consequences in the event of a lapse in responsibility.

- When kids experience consequences resulting from *their* choices (notice I am not using the word "punishment"), they learn quickly what type of behavior flies and what type doesn't. It is critical to introduce consequences when they fail to do a job, back talk, try to negotiate, or complain.

While writing this chapter, I had the uncomfortable (and fortunate) opportunity to take a deeper look at why my boys (ages 14 and 17) weren't stepping up with their chores, which my wife and I now call "responsibilities." They were talking back, making excuses, complaining, and sometimes cussing.

Through the mentoring I received from a buddy, I learned that I had put forth unclear expectations (with no agreements in place) and no consequences, which put the onus of the problem (and the blame) on *me*!

Once I put structure in place, my sons actually welcomed the clarity and discipline. They made positive shifts immediately and demonstrated a personal sense of pride and accomplishment for a job well done. I imagine this might go a long way in serving them in their life, especially when it comes to accountability.

The following set of suggestions may seem obvious. They are simple and effective ways in which to teach accountability and responsibility in your fathering:

- Set written agreements with your children, and include clear and written expectations and a clearly stated standard of completion and accountability (i.e., who does what and by when).

- Be sure you and your partner/spouse are on the same page.

- Set consequences for any failure to keep to the agreement(s), and get your kids involved in the process of creating responsibilities and accountability. (The leverage in my household is to take away their phone and/or social events.)

- In plain view, post the written agreements and consequences in your home for accountability.

- If agreements are broken, make sure to deliver the consequences; otherwise, you may continue to send the message that breaking the agreement is OK.

Notice your reactions to the process I've just described (both positive and negative), and consider them when constructing your Good Father Growth Plan.

Financial Responsibility

Your role as a father includes being aware of what you are modeling to your kids in the areas of spending, saving, investing, and managing money. Just as your parents' relationship with money shaped your relationship with money, the same goes for your kids. You pass on what you've learned and consciously teach them something new, both of which are very powerful.

Your responsibility is to be aware of your relationship with money and make mindful, positive changes your children may witness and follow. When it comes to fathering, doing your own work around money will serve you well.

Revisit Chapter 7, "Your Father," and review the questions there (Journal Entries #12 through #76).

Good Father Growth Plan

Now is the time to step up and put your learning into practice, and doing so requires a plan. Throughout this book, I have encouraged you to reflect on a variety of questions. By now, several insights may be swirling in your mind and written in your journal.

Now is the time to identify and use these insights to create new commitments and new behaviors you desire. As you do this, keep answering the question, "What kind of man do you see yourself becoming?"

Use your notes from this and previous chapters to fill out the following Good Father Growth Plan.

Building Awareness

✍ **JOURNAL ENTRY**

To what areas in your parenting do you need to bring your attention?

Examples:

- Improving the quality of your direct interactions with your children

- Being honest and honoring your wife in front of your children

- Being accountable in what you say and do, especially when it impacts others

Making New Commitments

✍️ JOURNAL ENTRY #139

What specific commitments will you make to support your growth as a parent?

Examples:

- Being more present with your kids with no competing focus

- Being respectful in communication with your wife

- Being authentic in all instances with your wife

- Modeling accountability and holding your kids accountable

Beginning New Behaviors

✍️ JOURNAL ENTRY #140

What new behaviors might you put into action to support your commitment(s)?

Examples:

- Turning off your phone when you are with your kids

- Scheduling time with your spouse and children

- Involving them in decisions of what to do together as a family

- Telling the truth to your wife even if it might upset her

- Verbally acknowledging your wife positively and with gratitude for one thing each day

- Taking responsibility and ownership for your actions when you are out of alignment and accountability with your wife and/or kids

Being Mindful of Old Beliefs and Behaviors

✑ **JOURNAL ENTRY #141**

To what old habits and behaviors do you desire to stay present and avoid?

Examples:

- Not having time because you are too busy

- Attempting to do too many things at once, which take you out of the present moment with your wife and children

- Yelling or raising your voice when you are upset

- Not speaking your truth about how you feel

- Not speaking your truth about what you desire from your wife and/or kids

- Using your parents' teaching of "Do what I say, not what I do"

Creating a Timeline to Measure Success

 JOURNAL ENTRY #142

By when will you complete your new commitments?

Examples:

- Acknowledging your wife at least once daily of your gratitude for something she did for the family, and ensuring your kids witness your action

- Agreeing to one activity (with the phone off) for two hours for one weekend a month to be fully present with your wife and/or kids

- Turning your phone off during meals

- Agreeing and arranging a date night with your partner

Asking for Ongoing Support

 JOURNAL ENTRY #143

Who might you ask to support you and hold you accountable?

Examples:

- Asking your wife to support you with behind-the-scenes feedback on your fathering

- Seeking out another father and a male friend with whom you might discuss your struggles

CHAPTER 15

The Good Partner/Husband

What are the energies that make up a good partner and husband?

Being a Good Husband by Your Own Design

When I got married for the first time, nobody offered me a handbook describing how to be a man in matrimony. I had no idea what it truly meant to be a "good husband." All I had was experience watching my dad be a husband to my mother and my grandfather be a husband to my grandmother. My hunch is that you didn't receive a handbook either and, if there *were* handbooks, there certainly would be several versions.

Ask six married men what being a good partner or husband is all about and you'll likely get six different answers. Then, ask six married *women* and you might get a few more answers! Everyone has specific ideas about what a good partner does and says, and it still feels like a guessing game for most men.

So what's a guy to do?

I offer this guide, which I used to establish a second marriage with my life partner. It has become a staple towards keeping my relationship with her healthy and stable. I offer my solution as a guide for your personal insight. My guide is flexible enough to allow you to interpret it in your own way.

At the end of this chapter, there is a Good Partner/Husband Growth Plan, which gives you the opportunity to craft a plan around areas on which you wish to concentrate and live out into action. *This is the shift from integration to manifestation.* Once you have integrated these new concepts into your way of thinking and awareness, you may then set out to manifest these concepts into your own reality by your own design. You might use it as a written "game plan" that you may decide to execute.

There are many available workshops designed specifically to assist men in learning how to be in a good relationship with a woman. As previously mentioned, Alison Armstrong's PAX workshops series is a great place to start. (For further information on other workshops, see "Menstuff.org" in the Resources section.)

The Four Male Archetypes

Different life situations and circumstances require different areas of focus for a man. When you are at work, you need a certain kind of focus and energy compared to when you are playing sports. When you are with your kids, you need a different kind of focus and energy compared to when you are with your buddies. In the same way, you might step into or embody several different types of male energy in your relationship with your partner or wife.

This male energy, known as an "archetype," is found in myths and stories across many cultures. It is a model of a person, personality, or behavior. In this chapter, I will discuss and relate to being a good husband with four male archetypes—king, warrior, magician, and lover—

created by by Robert Moore (Professor of Psychology, Chicago Theological Seminary) and Douglas Gillette (writer and counselor) in their book, *King, Warrior, Magician, Lover: Rediscovering the Archetypes of the Mature Masculine* (HarperSanFrancisco, 1990).

These four archetypes have a golden aspect (i.e., one to which you may aspire) as well as a shadow aspect (i.e., one that might hurt your women if you lack consciousness). The goal is to be aware of both aspects. The archetypes are templates upon which you can build and not necessarily strictly follow. As you read each description, you might notice how I reference the masculine core values, mentioned earlier in this book.

The King

Positive Personality Traits of the King (Adjusted for Modern Times)

- He takes full responsibility for his role as head of the household.

- He sees the big picture.

- He is sure of himself.

- He is wise and fair.

- He keeps the good of his family and community at the forefront of his mind.

- He is a leader.

- He is the male counterpart to his divine queen.

The King's Shadow Sides

- He is a tyrant, who rules by force, creating disharmony and chaos.

- He is an abdicator, who disappears, leaving his kingdom without a leader and creating disharmony and chaos.

Positive Actions You Might Take to Be the King in Your Relationship

- **Put your financial house in order.** To have a solid, healthy relationship with your partner or spouse, you need to have peace in the area of finances. The best approach is to have several conversations about commitments and expectations. Create agreements to make things clear and to prevent unspoken expectations.

  A good husband encourages financial autonomy from his partner or wife. Put another way, a good male partner or husband empowers the woman in his life, which includes her financial empowerment by maintaining partial responsibility for your portion of the finances.

- **Create and maintain a safe environment for your wife or partner.** Good communication with your partner or spouse is essential. Women typically relate by connecting, and it is imperative to be present and focused on her when you are talking and spending time together. It's a good idea to turn off your phones.

  A good husband listens from his heart and avoids leaping to solutions when his wife is venting to him about her problems. It is imperative as a husband to bring awareness to your emotional reactions, so you minimize their impact on the woman you love. I highly recommend "Understanding Women: Unlock the Mystery," provided by the PAX programs and founded by Alison Armstrong, which discusses in detail the subject of listening to women. (For more information about how to attend this workshop, see "Understanding Women" in the Resources section.)

- **Provide your household with the agreed-upon type of leadership.** Being the king is about your willingness and confidence to take risks and be responsible for your decisions and their consequences. Ask your partner or wife what kind of leadership model she desires to have with you, and listen to how and what she says. Many women prefer a collaborative model of leadership where both parties share important decisions instead of the old, patriarchal way where the man makes all the important decisions.

- **Be aware and stay present to any shadow behavior.** Notice if you want to run or go away, or exhibit tyrant or disappearing behavior, when you become overwhelmed. Stay on your seat—or "throne"—always.

Write down your answers to the following questions, and consider them when constructing your Good Partner/Husband Growth Plan.

✍ JOURNAL ENTRY #144

Do you have any financial agreements in place between you and your partner/spouse that outline responsibility? If so, what are they? If not, what areas might a financial agreement serve your relationship?

✍ JOURNAL ENTRY #145

How often do you and your partner/spouse set time aside to connect? Do you initiate connection? Who makes the plans? What might you like to see happen?

✍ JOURNAL ENTRY #146

Do you really listen to your partner/spouse? Do you provide her with the opportunity to "vent" while resisting the natural male inclination to fix?

✍ JOURNAL ENTRY #147

Are your emotional reactions containable? When an outburst occurs, why are you reacting? How do the feelings of shame, fear, and/or anger relate to your outburst?

✍ JOURNAL ENTRY #148

Are you aware of and do you own up to taking full responsibility for your hurtful behaviors? Do you work on minimizing these hurtful behaviors?

✍ JOURNAL ENTRY #149

If you continue to exhibit hurtful behaviors, are you willing to see someone to assist you in overcoming these tendencies?

✍ JOURNAL ENTRY #150

What causes you to feel as if you desire to disappear (or feel inclined to disappear) from your throne as king?

✍ JOURNAL ENTRY #151

Are there areas where your behavior is more like a tyrant?

The Warrior

Positive Personality Traits of the Warrior (Adjusted for Modern Times)

- He uses his power and energy to step into action and do what is necessary.

- He lives by a set of core values, his standards, and his code.

- He passionately commits to a purpose.

Being a warrior in today's world requires you to live a life of integrity, be accountable for your actions, and speak your truth. Simply translated, you do what you say you will do and, when you mess up, you own up to your mistake.

Warriors know how to use their power and manage it, especially with the women in their lives. Sometimes standing in your power and holding to your truth are exactly what your woman needs. When your wife or partner brings all her fury to you, stay connected to what you know is true inside you.

David Deida, well-known author of *The Way of the Superior Man* (Sounds True, 2006), says, "Stand in the storm of your woman and she will trust you—and desire you." My interpretation of this simply means to avoid taking her on and making it personal. Additionally, this statement suggests being firm in your position.

A warrior is able to balance his vitality, knowing when to shift from his immense power as a warrior and reduce or modulate it, which takes time to learn. Modulating your vitality means controlling the power and adapting its use and level relative to a given situation.

The Warrior's Shadow Sides

- He maybe a bully, who *over*utilizes his warrior energy.

- He maybe a coward, who *under*utilizes his warrior energy.

Positive Actions You Might Take to Be the Warrior in Your Relationship

Write down your answers to the following questions, and consider them when constructing your Good Partner/Husband Growth Plan.

✍ JOURNAL ENTRY #152

What projects in your household need your attention? What have you been putting off? (Hint: What has your partner/spouse been nagging you to do that you have been avoiding?) Being a warrior means seeing what needs to be done and getting it done without being asked.

✍ JOURNAL ENTRY #153

In what household projects are you out of integrity with your partner/wife? What things have you said you were going to do that still need to be done?

✍ JOURNAL ENTRY #154

Do you have a bullying or cowardly side that shows up in your relationship?

✍ JOURNAL ENTRY #155

What circumstances instigate your bulling or cowardly behavior?

✍ JOURNAL ENTRY #156

What would be some positive, opposite behaviors into which you might step?

✍ JOURNAL ENTRY #157

Under what circumstances do you give your power away to your partner/spouse?

✍ JOURNAL ENTRY #158

When does your power prove to be too much for your partner/spouse?

The Magician

Positive Personality Traits of the Magician (Adjusted for Modern Times)

- He is introspective.

- He takes time to look closely at himself.

- He is interested in his emotions.

- He is willing to experience his feelings to learn about himself.

- He uses his awareness for his emotional well-being and the well-being of others.

- He draws on deep, internal essential truths and resources to act consciously.

The Magician's Shadow Sides

- He is a know-it-all.

- He is a dummy.

Positive Actions You Might Take to Be the Magician in Your Relationship

The role of the magician requires you to transcend the specific behaviors you witnessed your father exhibit with your mother, as well as any behaviors you developed in reaction to your mother. By seeking awareness of old patterns and beliefs handed down from your parents or others in your life, you may transform your unconscious actions into conscious ones to support your relationships (as opposed to causing them harm).

Write down your answers to the following questions, and consider them when constructing your Good Partner/Husband Growth Plan.

✍ JOURNAL ENTRY #159

When there is conflict in your relationship, do you "manipulate" your partner/spouse to get your way?

✍ JOURNAL ENTRY #160

Does your "know-it-all" behavior disallow input from others?

✍ JOURNAL ENTRY #161

Do you resist introspection around your emotions and then continually make the same mistakes?

✍ JOURNAL ENTRY #162

Are you aware of the impact when you avoid looking within yourself?

✍ JOURNAL ENTRY #163

Do you know how it affects your partner/spouse? If so, list some ways.

✍ JOURNAL ENTRY #164

Are you aware of certain patterns showing up in your relationships that always end the same way?

✍ JOURNAL ENTRY #165

How willing are you to do whatever it takes to change the result?

The Lover

Positive Personality Traits of the Lover (Adjusted for Modern Times)

- He focuses on the realm of the senses: touch, sight, sound, taste, and smell.

- He is in tune with all aspects of beauty.

- He seeks unity and connection.

- He is opposed to all structures that isolate and separate.

- He is focused on making sure his world is organized around the ultimate purpose of love.

The lover is often the easiest to forget in the day-to-day responsibilities of being a husband and partner. The role of the lover is about seeing your partner/spouse for who she is, honoring her, creating a sacred space for the two of you, and resolving any issues right away to avoid accumulated resentment.

The lover is chivalrous and takes time to "create a safe environment" to connect with his partner. Being the lover requires maturity, patience, passion, and honor. Meaningful acts that you do for your wife send her messages of being worthy of your attention, time, and effort—with no attachment to an outcome.

The Lover's Shadow Sides

- He is an addict, who constantly searches for fulfillment (a woman here and a woman there, with no satisfaction).

- He is impotent, chronically depressed, sexually inactive, and cut off from the world.

Positive Actions You Might Take to Be the Lover in Your Relationship

Write down your answers to the following questions, and consider them when constructing your Good Partner/Husband Growth Plan.

✍ JOURNAL ENTRY #166

What do you love about your partner/spouse? What makes her unique?

✍ JOURNAL ENTRY #167

How do you honor your partner/spouse?

✍ JOURNAL ENTRY #168

Do you make any effort to have special time for just the two of you? If so, how often?

✍ JOURNAL ENTRY #169

Do any of the lover's shadow sides resonate with you? If so, do you have enough of a concern to address them with a professional?

✍ JOURNAL ENTRY #170

Do you have regular check-in talks to see how your partner/spouse is doing? If so, how often?

Good Partner/Husband Growth Plan

It's time to step up and put your learning into practice, and doing so requires a plan. Throughout this book, I have encouraged you to reflect on a variety of questions. By now, several insights may be swirling in your mind and in your journal.

It's time to use these insights to create new commitments and new behaviors. As you do this, keep answering the question, "What kind of man do you see yourself becoming?"

Using your notes from this and previous chapters, respond to the below questions by writing in your journal to create the following Good Partner/Husband Growth Plan. Consider the four archetypes—king, warrior, magician, and lover—when you are making your plan.

Building Awareness

 JOURNAL ENTRY #171

What areas in your relationship need your attention?

Examples:

- Getting better financial agreements around your budget

- Talking less and listening more

- Shifting your anger in conflict

- Seeing things that need to get done ahead of time so you may plan to do them

- Modulating your power around your wife/partner

- Experiencing your emotions

- Consciously honoring your wife/partner

Making New Commitments

✍️ JOURNAL ENTRY #172

For what commitments are you willing to be held accountable?

Examples:

- Having a monthly financial meeting defining roles/responsibilities/budget

- Working on your emotions and power in a men's group

- Arranging a date night once a month to honor your wife

- Discussing projects that need to get done early in the week, so your wife may do what she wants to do for herself during the weekend

Beginning New Behaviors

✍️ JOURNAL ENTRY #173

What do your commitments look like "in action"?

Examples:

- Being more introspective about your feelings

- Going into action and getting things done without having to be asked

- Making a conscious effort to listen and not interrupt

- Checking budget expenditures with your wife/partner

Being Mindful of Old Beliefs and Behaviors

✍️ JOURNAL ENTRY #174

Of what do you need to stay aware that may take you off course?

Examples:

- Avoiding phrases such as, "It can wait until tomorrow"

- Avoiding phrases such as, "I'm the provider, and she does every-thing related to the home"

- Raising your voice

Creating a Timeline to Measure Success

✍️ JOURNAL ENTRY #175

What timeframe might you use to monitor your progress?

Examples:

- Checking in on a monthly basis around the topics of measuring success

- Coming to a mutual agreement around the progress

- Determining your success through feedback from your wife/partner and/or a men's group

Asking for Ongoing Support

✍ JOURNAL ENTRY #176

Who might support you in being accountable to your commitments?

Examples:

- Joining a men's group

- Asking your best friend

- Asking your wife/partner

CHAPTER 16

The Masculine Leader

What kind of leader in your personal and professional life do you aspire to be?

Your Version of Leadership in Your Life

Many books, articles, and blogs focus on leadership in the workplace, and often chronicle great corporate and political leaders of the past; however, the rare book or blog speaks to what it means to lead in your life as a man—right now, *today.*

What does leadership look like for the rest of us who don't have the entire world as our stage? Where are your opportunities? What is being asked of you? What is at stake?

In order to answer these questions, you need to understand what leadership is and is not. Many personal and business life experiences have given you glimpses of various styles of leadership, which have allowed you to form opinions and beliefs and create behaviors that shape you as a man. By being aware of what you believe, and modeling that leadership behavior, you may construct a powerful leadership style to serve your everyday life and work life.

What do the words "lead" and "leader" mean to you? You use outer definitions (i.e., ones you might look up in a dictionary) and inner definitions (i.e., ones you actually formed under the leadership of someone else) in your daily life as a man.

I want to talk about the inner definitions because they are more powerful. Your inner definitions of the words "lead" and "leader" comprise what you know intellectually, your beliefs about leadership, and your experiences with people in positions of power.

At the end of this chapter, there is a Masculine Leadership Growth Plan, which gives you the opportunity to craft a plan around your leadership and about which areas you wish to concentrate and live out into action. *This is the shift from integration to manifestation.* Once you have integrated these new concepts into your way of thinking and awareness, you may then set out to manifest these concepts into your own reality by your own design. You might use it as a written "game plan" that you may decide to execute.

Here are some questions you may answer and journal to determine your inner definitions about being a leader:

✍ JOURNAL ENTRY #177

Was your father a leader? Have you had good bosses? Have you had terrible bosses? Did the people who were supposed to lead you offer support or did they have a hands-off approach? Has any leader in your life experience inspired you? If so, how? What leader in your life experience may have inspired you? If so, how?

Questions like these begin the exploration of why you think and act the way you do, and why you believe the way you do with respect to leaders and leadership; in other words, they define your personal definition of leadership.

Exploring your personal definition offers you an opportunity to consciously re-craft your vision of leadership (and ultimately your behaviors) and avoid being unconsciously led by something old and outdated—with an emphasis on the words "conscious" and "unconscious."

"Lead" and "Leader" Are Charged Words

A "charged" word has a dictionary definition *and* connects you to your past. For example, words like "money," "sex," "power," "love," "religion," "politics," "equality," "family," and "God" all have personal meanings, demonstrating more to the word than the definition. It includes your experience(s) with the word and its representation to you.

Knowing a word is charged gives you a leg up because it allows you to be aware of how your experiences with that word influence your current perception of it. This relates directly to leadership.

Just as you learned from Fatherly Influence #5, "How your dad dealt with money and influenced your views and relationship with money" (Chapter 7, "Your Father"), you may become conscious to the leadership influences of your past and the role they play in your present day. This allows you to ferret out what's working—and what's not working—on your path to becoming a powerful masculine leader.

The Inside/Outside Process

The Inside/Outside Process is an exercise that helps you develop a solid definition of the word "leader." It probes how your experiences around leadership have shaped your beliefs, behaviors, and ultimately your style and presence.

First, look up the words "lead" and "leader" in the dictionary and read the definitions carefully. Then, take the time, eliminate any distractions, and write down the answers to the following questions in your journal:

✍ JOURNAL ENTRY #178

Look inward at your concepts, visions, or models, and define what the words "lead" and "leader" mean to you. Do these words trigger or remind you of anything (positive or negative)? If so, what?

✍ JOURNAL ENTRY #179

Consider what general rules or beliefs you hold about leadership resulting from your experiences. Negative examples might be, "All leaders are out for themselves" or "Leaders can't be trusted." A positive example might be, "Leaders are people with insight and good ideas." Write down your beliefs and rules from your experiences.

✍ JOURNAL ENTRY #180

Consider how these beliefs and rules show up in your life now. Based on these beliefs, do any behaviors accompany these beliefs? If you hold that all leaders are "out for themselves," what do you do because of this belief? If you hold the belief that "leaders can't be trusted," a corresponding behavior might be, "I don't get behind and support leaders because I don't trust them." Do these beliefs help you? Do they limit you?

✍ JOURNAL ENTRY #181

To the extent that your beliefs are limiting, attempt to reframe them more positively and create new beliefs to support your leadership. For example, you might change "Leaders can't be trusted" to "Some leaders can be trusted."

JOURNAL ENTRY #182

Recall any men in your life who demonstrated positive leadership attributes. Maybe the man was a coach, a teacher, a scout leader, an uncle, or even your father. What was it about this man that you associate with being a good leader? What were his behaviors? What did those behaviors say about him as a man?

Return to the dictionary and choose the definitions most resonate with you; in other words, the one you see most in yourself. You now have your "outer definition."

 JOURNAL ENTRY #183

Revisiting Journal Entries #181 and #182, choose the positively reframed beliefs about leadership (Journal Entry #181). What positive behaviors might accompany these beliefs?

 JOURNAL ENTRY #187

On a new page in your journal, list the belief(s) and the behavior(s).

 JOURNAL ENTRY #188

Look over the list you created in Journal Entry #182 to see if anything new and/or affirming shows up. If so, write it down.

 JOURNAL ENTRY #189

Craft a concise statement of your inner and outer understanding of the words "lead" and "leader."

My outer definition of "lead" is "guide on a way by going in advance." One of my former beliefs around leadership was that leaders are highly visible people. I believed leaders had to be outgoing and tell people what to do.

I have come to realize that leaders don't actually need to be "out in front," giving people instructions. Instead, they might model the behavior they wish to see and communicate it in ways to support or replace giving orders.

My inner/outer definition of "leadership" is "guiding others through your actions in both subtle and obvious ways." A core component of leading requires a willingness to go forward and stand for something, so others may do this as well.

Now that you are more aware of your inner and outer definitions of leadership, let's look at the masculine core values that drive your behavior, so you may bring them into your personal leadership model.

Masculine Core Values and Leadership

Each man has inner and outer definitions of leadership as well as masculine core values. Together, they form masculine leadership.

Here are the masculine core values defined in Chapter 3, "Starting Your Journey":

- **Vitality:** Having energy, and being strong and active

- **Authenticity:** Being true to your personality, spirit, or character, and speaking to that truth

- **Honor:** Being honest and fair, and doing the right thing, which includes being honest with yourself and others

- **Integrity:** Displaying in word and deed that you are committed to the values, beliefs, and principles you claim to hold.

- **Accountability:** Taking full responsibility for your words, choices, and actions, and their consequences—intended or not

This potent combination of masculine core values, plus a conscious understanding of your definition of leadership (both inner and outer), provide the opportunity to lead through your words (i.e., how you communicate) and through your choices and actions.

Words and Communication

Here are some examples of how words are one of your most powerful tools as a masculine leader:

- Speaking words from your character reflects authenticity.

- Having integrity means that your words match your actions.

- You demonstrate honor by speaking your truth (i.e., honoring yourself) and asking others to do the same (i.e., honoring others).

As a masculine leader, avoid underestimating the impact of your words, and never underestimate the power you have in how you see others. This applies to your marriage, your community, your children, and your workplace. You are a man and a leader, and they are the same.

Choices and Actions

All masculine leaders have difficult choices as a matter of routine. When making difficult choices, the masculine leader draws from his core values, using them as an internal guide upon which he bases his decisions.

Vitality is a very important core value because internal fortitude helps a man make difficult decisions, which are certain to have consequences. Put another way, if you upset some people due to your decisions, you need to have the strength to stay strong when they are upset.

Your words and actions are forms of communication. As a masculine leader, what you do, how you do it, and to whom you do it are all forms of modeling because those around you always scrutinize your words and actions.

For example, if your actions don't align with your words, an integrity challenge arises for which you need to be held accountable. It is rare to find a leader who takes full accountability rather than offer "the story" as to why "it" wasn't his fault.

Here are some questions to answer and write down about your masculine core values in the context of leadership:

✍️ JOURNAL ENTRY #190

Where are your values self-evident and functioning?

✍️ JOURNAL ENTRY #191

Where are your values lacking?

✍️ JOURNAL ENTRY #192

Are there any areas in your leadership (at home or in business) resulting in consequences that you need to clean up?

✍️ JOURNAL ENTRY #193

What values might you use to guide you?

🖊 JOURNAL ENTRY #194

How do values expressed by other leaders shape your own role and behavior as a leader?

🖊 JOURNAL ENTRY #195

How do you treat others over whom you have power or authority?

🖊 JOURNAL ENTRY #196

Where in your various roles (e.g., husband, father, businessman, or friend) might your leadership skills improve?

Leadership opportunities exist all around you, every day, if you choose to be open to looking for and receiving them. Whether you are a father, a husband, an ex-husband, a real male friend, or a businessman (or all of the above), you have leadership choices. You may need to decide where in your life your leadership is being beckoned.

Masculine Leadership Growth Plan

It's time to step up and put your learning into practice, and doing so requires a plan. Leading in your life may have many areas of focus (e.g., parenting, marriage, community, religious organization, or a cause in which you believe). It's up to you to decide which area needs you the most and you desire to improve.

Throughout this book, I have encouraged you to reflect on a variety of questions. By now, several insights may be swirling in your mind and in your journal. It's time to use these insights to create new commitments and new behaviors. As you do this, keep answering the question,

"What area of your life is calling forth your masculine leader, and who do you see yourself being in this journey?"

Use your notes from this and previous chapters to fill out the following Masculine Leadership Growth Plan.

Building Awareness

 **JOURNAL ENTRY #197**

What areas in your leadership need your attention?

Examples:

- Supporting your wife into her leadership

- Seeking opportunities to lead by your actions

- Encouraging others into their leadership role

Making New Commitments

 **JOURNAL ENTRY #198**

What commitments are you willing to make?

Examples:

- Assigning responsibility to another team member and following their lead

- Making attempts to empower others into their leadership role

Beginning New Behaviors

 JOURNAL ENTRY #199

What do your commitments look like "in action"?

Examples:

- Empowering others by giving them the opportunity to lead

- Taking on a lesser role in support of another's success

Being Mindful of Old Beliefs and Behaviors

 JOURNAL ENTRY #200

Of what do you need to stay aware that might take you off course?

Examples:

- Accepting the fact that it's easy to tell others what to do and denying them the opportunity to step up

- Understanding that you don't have all the answers, and that someone wins and someone loses

Creating a Timeline to Measure Success

 JOURNAL ENTRY #201

What timeframe will you use to monitor your progress?

Examples:

- Over the next 90 days, seeking honest feedback from your spouse and family members in the areas to which you have put your attention (e.g., picking up after yourself, taking out the trash, and speaking respectfully to all family members)

- Picking a project, which can be completed at work and which requires somebody else's leadership, and your participation can be completed in a month

Asking for Ongoing Support

 JOURNAL ENTRY #202

Who will support you in being accountable to your commitments?

Examples:

- Receiving support from your wife for matters of the home

- Seeking a work peer or mentor whom you respect to give you feedback

CHAPTER 17

Real Male Friendships

How do you create, foster, and enhance real male friendships?

Is It Something You Want?

Do you have good male friends? Are you able to rely on any men in your life to speak the truth to you, to support you when you need help, and to be together when you desire to have fun? If you do, you have paid attention to and made time to cultivate these friendships over time. If you avoided this commitment, you are like many men in our society with limited male friends who may lack the ability to be supportive.

Deep down, men yearn for real male friendships. They require effort—especially when you are also trying just as hard to juggle the pressures of a career and family life.

Hollywood sees these yearnings before we do. Movies and TV shows about male friendships continue to proliferate, and the "buddy movie" is still alive and well at the box office. Hollywood has coined a new term—"bromance"—to poke fun at two heterosexual guys who have a deep relationship. Most of these movies only scratch the surface and often parody the awkwardness of heterosexual men being together. Recently, a few movies have taken a deeper look at authentic relationships between heterosexual men, and they still have much to learn … and explore.

How do you cultivate real male friends? Where do you meet them? How does it work? First, let's consider the criteria for having a real male friend.

Definition of Real Male Friends

What is *your* definition of a "real male friend"? Many men just take what they get, and limit their definition to a drinking buddy or someone they call when they feel down.

I invite you to consider a more supportive definition. To me, a real male friend is someone:

- Who has your back

- Who challenges you to be better

- Who tells you the truth

- Who calls you out on your stuff and holds you accountable

- Who loves you for who you are, despite your shortcomings

- Who makes you want to be a better person

- With whom you may laugh, cry, be angry, and appreciate

- On whom you may rely

- With whom you have fun

You may notice these attributes looking a lot like the kind you might use to describe your ideal female partner. They are indeed the same because a real male friend (in my world) is someone with whom you cultivate a deep and sometimes lifelong relationship.

Still, depending on what part of the country you live in or what country you come from, you will encounter different cultural views on male relationships. In some areas of the world, straight men hold hands. In other areas (like the United States), straight men are expected only to shake hands and never hold hands; any gesture other than a handshake or a quick slap on the back may be considered an expression of homosexuality.

Male hugging is a gray area even though it has slowly made its way into the mainstream. It currently involves a combination of handshakes, hugs, and backslapping, with the newest form being a "handshake hug."

Positive Results and Challenges

Here is a list of some positive results I experienced from knowing and spending time with real male friends:

- Being involved with a rich, rewarding community of men

- Having lots of fun, which may rejuvenate you

- Having a safe place to work through your stuff as a man

- Relying on someone whom you trust

- Having someone who holds you to a higher standard

- Achieving a balanced energy that supports you in your marriage and/or in intimate relationships

In addition to the positives, relationship challenges may also confront you. Expect some unresolved issues with your mom, dad, or adolescence to show up; you might even have your homophobia button pushed (if you have one).

Still, the benefits of having real male friends may thoroughly outweigh the challenges. Don't take my word for it—experience it yourself!

Why Cultivate Real Male Friendships?

To Find Strength in Numbers

Being isolated didn't help you deal with your wake-up call, and it won't help you after you've answered it. Having support is a lifetime thing.

No one expects you to be at your best or do everything by yourself. Sometimes, you desire a different perspective and a different set of ideas and resources that may come from another guy. Men know what it's like to struggle as a man, and one of us may have already learned a lesson that is exactly what someone else needs to hear.

Put simply, we men might accomplish more and be more effective in our parenting, leadership, and relationships if we stick together.

To Fill a Void

As a kid and a teenager, some of my best moments were with my guy friends. For some reason, these times with men decrease as we get older, and our need for male camaraderie and connection is always present. Having real male friends fills a void separate from that of female friends.

To Challenge You to Be Better

My own experience of having close real male friends has affected all areas of my life. For example:

- My male friends share in my responsibility of raising my sons to be men.

- They challenge me to be a better leader.

- They stand for the success of my relationship with my wife.

- Being with them gives me balance and an appreciation for time with my wife.

- They give me a place where I may do my men's work, so I am able to be a better man.

To Have Fun

This aspect is often the most overlooked! You are always young enough to have fun. Having fun keeps your inner youth alive, and sometimes being irreverent is just as important as being reverent.

I routinely plan outings with my guy friends because it rejuvenates me (and directly affects my fathering and my ability to be a good husband). After time away with the guys, I have a new appreciation of coming back into the family fold.

Finding Real Male Friends

Finding real male friends starts with being one. This is where your masculine core values enter the picture. Think about your values and answer the question, "Do any of your guy friends hold similar masculine core values?" Maybe you work with some guys whom you like or share a hobby with a few guys in your neighborhood.

I have learned that, when I am more authentic, truthful, honest, and accountable, the guys I'm with usually follow the same behavior. Start having real male friends by using your courage and vulnerability with the men to whom you already feel a connection. Take a risk. For every risk, there is a reward. I advise you to discern on a case-by-case base what level of these attributes you reveal and share based on where the other man is in his growth.

Real male friends may come from every walk of life. If you don't have social places where you meet guys, consider taking up a sport or hobby that supports natural gatherings. If you don't have a lot of men in your life, which is not uncommon, reach out and take a risk by putting yourself into new groups of men to share your hobbies, beliefs, spiritual practice, and maybe even volunteer interests.

Where might you find guys with masculine core values similar to yours? Maybe there is church or synagogue, a civic group (like a Rotary Club), or some other group that might put you in contact with other men. All kinds of men's groups are sprouting up, so follow your interests and find out what's happening near you.

Find men who are open to learning about themselves and becoming better men. When you find men on their own path, perhaps the same masculine core values may resonate with both of you and be a foundation for a good relationship. Approach some of your existing friends and share your intention to cultivate more solid male friendships. They might want the same thing.

Guidelines to Becoming a Real Male Friend

Being a real male friend is not a precise science. Here are some guidelines you might follow:

- Be the kind man you want to see in others.

- Be authentic.

- Tell the truth.

- Listen to understand.

- Be accountable for your agreements. Let your actions do the talking.

- Own your part in any disagreement. The cleanest and best way to end a disagreement is to acknowledge your part in it. This models behavior for the other man and, with luck, he might do the same.

- Hold your guy friends accountable.

- Ask permission to offer feedback, if you have it. Giving feedback without permission means that your feedback is unsolicited and might be a projection.

- Honor any man where he is in his men's journey. Remember: His men's journey and Your Men's Journey are different.

- Ask for what you need.

- Have lots of fun.

Navigating Male Friendships While Respecting Your Partner or Spouse

Men are notorious for trying many approaches around spending time with the buddies, the dudes, and the guys.

None of the below approaches are long-term solutions in dealing with your partner or spouse:

- **"Honey, is it OK with you if I go out with the guys this Saturday?"** By asking if it's all right for you to spend time with your buddies, you are essentially asking permission, giving your power away, and making your partner/spouse your mother, which she probably despises. This communication dynamic is a turnoff to women.

- **"Honey, I'm going out with my buddies and I will be back later."** This version is dictatorial and avoids a collaborative discussion to get to some kind of mutually workable end. This is a unilateral statement and prevents your partner/spouse from supporting you in what you desire.

- **"Honey, I will be back in a few hours …" (and you show up five hours later).** This disrespectful behavior is a recipe for disaster. You definitely reap the repercussions—perhaps immediately and certainly later.

- **You are silent.** If you leave without asking and without discussion, it exhibits very macho behavior and avoids contribution to a long-lasting, mutually beneficial relationship. This behavior is the opposite of what a "good husband" does.

With the exception of the last example, I can honestly say I did all of the above. Once I answered my wake-up call and changed my behavior, the simplicity of how to handle this situation suddenly became clear.

Here are some specific guidelines in successfully navigating male friendships while respecting your partner or spouse:

- Think about what might be a win-win scenario with respect to chores, responsibilities, kids, and your partner's needs. Think about who might do what and by when, and do this ahead of time so it may be easy for your partner/spouse to give you her blessing.

- Communicate your desire to spend time with your guy friends and tell your partner/spouse you want to talk about how you want to make it work for everyone involved. Let your partner/spouse know it is a collaborative process with a goal of meeting everyone's needs.

- Stick to the terms of the agreement and over deliver, if possible.

- Show some form of appreciation when you come home.

Here are some examples of a conscious man's approach:

- They take care of business, their families, and themselves.

- They collaborate with their partners.

- They avoid asking permission like a little boy.

- They avoid making unilateral decisions.

- They keep their agreements and stay in integrity.

- They use the collaborative approach, unlike the old macho model. They are considerate, creative, and mutual.

Ideas and Action Steps to Find Real Male Friendships

Finding and cultivating real male friendships take time and effort. To give you a little push, I've put together a list of ideas and some action steps to start you on your way. Be diligent and patient, and have a healthy sense of humor about it all.

- Watch the movie, "I Love You, Man." This movie might make you laugh, and it may make you feel better about the whole male-friend thing. It does a great job of showcasing the do's and don'ts of finding real male friends. It highlights the awkwardness of trying to find friends the way the main character goes about it. You may or may not choose to follow his lead!

- Review "Positive Results and Challenges," above, and be honest with yourself if any/all of the potential positive results resonate with you. Notice any reluctance to believe any positives and get curious about what is behind any potential blockages.

- Review Chapter 7, "Your Father," specifically in the area of relating to men, to see if any of your "stuff" with your dad is coloring your perception. Recognize this as old stuff, and answer the question, "What might you desire in an ideal relationship with a male friend?"

- Consider your existing pool of male friends and recall your masculine core values. Do any of these male friends strike you as someone whom you may like to know better? Do you already trust any of them? Make a list of these guys (maybe there is just one).

- If you lack close guys in your life, maybe a woman in your life knows of good men. Share with her why you are pursuing healthy male relationships. Describe your masculine core values, and ask if she knows other men with the same values. It really helps to share a hobby or similar physical activity.

- When you meet with a guy in your sphere or are introduced to someone new, share that you are interested in having real male friends in your life. Plan some time to get to know each other and have fun.

- Share your values and tell him what's important to you. Ask him to share his values, and find out if he is interested in continuing the conversation.

- Share some of the positive results you are looking for. See if they are important to him. If you are comfortable, share the nature of your wake-up call. Your ability to speak frankly and honestly may set the bar for what happens next.

- If you are interested in becoming friends after a couple of get-togethers, share the guidelines (see "Guidelines to Becoming a Real Male Friend," above) to see if they are acceptable to him.

- If you are married or in a relationship, be mindful of how this friendship affects it (see "Navigating Male Friendships While Respecting Your Partner or Spouse," above).

Do all of the above, consciously knowing at some point there will be relationship challenges, miscommunication, and crossed wires. Your stuff may show up, and so might your guy friends' stuff, too.

Stay in the fire. It's worth your effort!

CHAPTER 18

Navigating a Conscious Divorce

How do you survive the experience of divorce?

Navigating the "Interior" of Divorce

In my view, there are two complimentary ways to navigate a divorce and both are important; unfortunately, one is often overlooked and not confronted. The first, which I refer to as "outer" navigation, is all about the externals, such as laws, money, custody, and marriage settlement agreements; however, the train often comes off the track with "inner" navigation.

Many professionals make good careers from helping people with outer navigation (e.g., attorneys, certified public accountants, child custody specialists, and divorce consultants). The expertise of most of these professionals stops with outer navigation.

Inner navigation is about:

- The ability (or failure) to recognize emotions, to manage them when they come up, and to be aware of how they might affect you and the people around you

- Being able to stay present to what's happening inside you with respect to yourself, your ex, your kids, and your new partner, if you have one

- Thinking ahead, so you make decisions based on your values and what is fair, and avoid your fired-up sense of retribution or powerless resignation

I'm talking about how to take the high road, the less traveled and more difficult road. If you do this, you will be able to hold your head high and have integrity with yourself and with other people. You may be a model for other men and, if you have kids, you might be a grounding influence for them.

More importantly, many men lack the realization that how they choose to go *through* the divorce process sets the tone for life *after* the process. If you have kids, you are still going to be co-parenting with your former spouse for a long time to come. With or without kids, taking the high road may actually help you heal and may serve you in your next relationship.

Put another way, how honorably or dishonorably you exit this relationship will definitely shape your relationships in the future.

Guiding Principles in Navigating a Conscious Divorce

The following principles are guidelines to help you on this difficult journey to be a better man, and move through your divorce with integrity and foresight.

These principles might assist you, even if:

- You or your spouse has addiction problems.

- Your wife has left you and desires to end the relationship.

- Your wife had an affair and she wants to leave.

- You had an affair and want to reconcile, and your wife is moving on.

- Despite counseling, both of you desire to exit the relationship.

- There is emotional abuse, and it's best to end the relationship.

- You have anger issues on which you are working.

Take Ownership

As a man, you have the power to influence the divorce process so it is more collaborative and less ugly. This requires taking a deeper look at your contribution to the demise of your marriage, and taking responsibility for your part in it.

- Perhaps you lacked presence.

- Perhaps sufficient time and effort lacked in the relationship.

- Maybe you fell out of love and kept it to yourself.

- Maybe you were afraid to stand up for yourself.

- Maybe you got married for all the wrong reasons.

Whatever your case is, you played a part in what happened to your marriage, and the sooner you come to terms with this realization, the better. Taking ownership goes a long way to making this process easier. It also helps you in your next relationship.

Simply put, you have to take ownership for your part in the failure of *this* relationship to avoid making the same mistakes in your *next* relationship.

In Chapter 7, "Your Father," you discovered how your father treated your mother and how his behavior may have influenced the way in which you treat women. In Chapter 8, "Your Mother," you looked deeper into your relationship with your mother, and explored how any unhealed wounds from her relationship might show up in your marriage.

Taking ownership requires you to take responsibility for behaviors that may have contributed to the relationship breakdown. By doing this, you avoid the pointless trap of the blame game.

I suggest the following steps to assist you in taking ownership of your behavior. Write down the answers in your journal.

✍ JOURNAL ENTRY #203

What areas might you acknowledge in your marriage where you avoided giving it your all? Now might be a good time to review the four male archetypes of king, warrior, magician, and lover (Chapter 15, "The Good Partner/Husband") to see where you may have culpability. You might get some clues from reviewing the places where your former spouse expressed dismay.

Consider the impact this behavior had on both of you, and ultimately your marriage. Forgive yourself for your shortcomings. At this point, it's more important how you act going forward than being stuck on a past event. Resolve to improve your efforts with new commitments to align with your masculine core values and the four male archetypes.

When the time is right (and be sure to consult your attorney), communicate the behaviors for which you are taking ownership, preferably in a letter to your former spouse or in person, without attachment to any outcome. Discernment on your part as to whether she is capable of receiving it is required.

The alternative for the sake of your process is to write a letter that you will never send. Doing so might begin the process of self-forgiveness and, if she is capable of receiving and reading the letter, it may very well rebuild trust with her, which will go a long way in your co-parenting relationship if children are involved.

However, she may not be ready to hear it right away. If this is the case, your actions and words going forward need to be in integrity with your new sense of responsibility. Your actions have to speak louder than your words. Trust me on this: There may be many opportunities to behave with accountability and integrity, exhibiting this new behavior. These actions speak the loudest.

I offer the following questions to support you in bringing awareness to your old behaviors and their consequences, so you eventually step into a new relationship where you may make different choices with your newfound awareness.

First, go back to the section on the Five Fatherly Influences (Chapter 7, "Your Father") and review your answers to those questions. Then, take the time, eliminate any distractions, and write down the answers to the following questions in your journal:

✍️ JOURNAL ENTRY #204

Specifically consider your answer to Fatherly Influence #4, "How your father related to your mom." What behaviors have you repeated that you saw growing up?

✍️ JOURNAL ENTRY #205

Did these behaviors contribute to the demise of your marriage? If so, how?

✏️ JOURNAL ENTRY #206

With this new awareness, what changes in your behavior do you want to make?

Seek a Win-Win for All Parties

Any time a marriage heads in the direction of a divorce, emotions may easily get the best of everyone and bring out the worst. If you have something else in place, you prevent emotional reactions from becoming the only force guiding your actions and influencing your decisions. In many divorces, a shared value of win-win is missing, which functions as a guiding principle on both parties mutually agree when it comes to making big decisions.

For example, when my former wife and I divorced, we agreed to create the best environment possible for our children and support each other in our new lives. This principle influenced everything (e.g., where and how close we would live and how we would handle custody issues).

When it came time for holidays and vacations, we had a shared vision. We wanted to put the kids first and build upon ourselves in the process. This principle reflected our core values and kept us from making decisions that might have unnecessarily hurt each other and our kids. Twelve years later, my former wife and I still adhere to this guiding principle.

Developing a mutually agreed upon, value-driven principle is completely possible and difficult. Even if mutuality isn't happening in your relationship with your ex right now, you might be the one to start it by changing *your* behavior and letting your masculine core values drive your actions. Better yet, consider taking the lead by asking your ex-spouse what *she* needs. If you find that taking the lead is a strange or uncomfortable idea, perhaps you avoided this action in your marriage.

If you have kids, it's important to understand that you are still a family. Most people forget this. It is also worth noting that your family includes you and your former spouse as well as her new partner and your new partner. All of you need support.

 JOURNAL ENTRY #207

How might your masculine core values from Chapter 3, "Starting Your Journey," serve you in your dissolution process?

 JOURNAL ENTRY #208

If you have kids, what is the optimal win-win scenario for them? Consider things such as time with dad/mom, ease of transition, predictable schedules, and having a voice when they are in their adolescent stage.

 JOURNAL ENTRY #209

What is important to you?

 JOURNAL ENTRY #210

What might be your win-win?

 JOURNAL ENTRY #211

What do you imagine putting in place now so the future is healthier for all parties involved?

Be Conscious with Custody

Conscious custody is all about being present with your children when they are with you. It's about being empathic to what is going on for your kids as well as to yourself. The disruption of the divorce is traumatic enough on kids, and the back and forth of custody arrangements may even be more disorienting for them. Your children need you more than you realize, and they need your presence and attention.

Keeping in mind all you have learned about the Five Fatherly Influences, and that the role of the father in a child's life strongly influences their self-esteem and confidence, decide what level of involvement you want to have in your children's lives.

When considering this, there are many single-parent "reality factors" to consider:

- **Parenting by yourself.** When the kids are with you, you are 100% responsible for their well-being.

- **Cooking and cleaning.** If they are living with you, feeding them requires you to shop, cook, and clean.

- **Doing laundry.** Kids' clothes, sheets, and towels need to be washed and folded. *You* do that (unless they are old enough to help).

- **Being present.** Being home with your kids when you have custody requires you to be with them. This means being conscious of your presence with them versus caught up in your work.

- **Providing rides.** It is your job to pick them up and drive them places.

- **Entertaining.** Kids like to have fun and do things.

- **Using diplomacy.** When you are with your kids, they will scrutinize your actions and words. How you speak about your former wife, how the two of you make parenting decisions, and even how the two of you demonstrate support in your children's activities all need conscious thought and attention. As long as you have children, you and your former spouse are in a co-parenting relationship.

When it comes to custody, being conscious requires a full understanding of what's most important to the well-being of your children, what new things will be required of you, and how these new requirements will impact your life and the life of your children.

Being conscious might require you to transcend some of your old pain and old ways for the sake of everyone's healing—including yours. This is certainly a road less traveled, and I assure you that a mature, masculine man is capable of seeing the big picture and acting on what's best *for everyone.*

The range of custody agreements may span from no custody to complete custody with one parent. Custody is a decision that is hard to undo, so make this choice carefully. You get out of it what you put into it. At the time of my divorce, I only imagined 50% custody. It ended up being 45%, and I struggle with this decision to this day.

For those of you in the throes of an adversarial process around custody, I encourage you to remember life as a kid, and recall the importance of having your father in your life. If your father was absent in your life, use the pain of his absence as a motivator to do whatever it takes to be in your children's lives when it comes to custody. If your father was in your life, then you know how important and valuable your role is. It is worth standing up for this.

When staying consciously present, the opportunity is to stand up for something important … like your kids.

See the Big Picture

There is a "big picture" around custody issues. It involves you, your kids, their emotional well-being, and your happiness. Even though you may be very hurt right now, there will be a time when the pain of this process will be over. Keep this endpoint in mind, and imagine what life will be like for everyone involved as you make your current decisions.

Adhere to your guiding principle or personal values, and allow something larger (other than retribution or guilt) to guide your decisions. For example, in my divorce, I made sure the proceeds of the divorce allowed my former wife to purchase a home in the same county, so my kids remained in the same school.

My guiding principle was to minimize the disruption in my children's lives. I knew it would benefit my kids most to have my former wife remain a stay-at-home mom, so our alimony arrangement made this possible.

This may fly in the face of what many of you have learned (i.e., get the most out of your divorce and avoid being "taken to the cleaners"). I encourage you to consider the big picture and the details of what you will be living with day to day once your divorce is over.

This one example isn't the only way to see the big picture. I know men who felt so badly about the demise of their marriage that they gave up advocating for their future well-being. The decisions made at the time of their divorce made eventual happiness and the possibility of a healthy life (e.g., relationship and finances) difficult after the divorce.

In order to set the stage for your conscious divorce, I strongly encourage you to establish some sort of collaborative process now, so you may create a model for all future discussions. This will lead to amicable and equitable resolutions to financial issues that will inevitably arise.

Why is this smart? Most men going through a divorce waste emotional energy, time, and money on attorneys. They feel hurt and let their reactions drive their decisions and actions.

More insidiously, most men don't realize that, without some way of collaborating, they will end up giving the power of making extremely important decisions, which have long-term effects, to a judge, who in most instances will make these decisions without intimately knowing the family.

If you are in a situation where your soon-to-be former spouse is acting irrationally, I recommend taking a stance of fairness. Recall what your wife was like when you married her (before the irrational behavior). Imagine what might be fair to her. Remember: The kids' needs are first, followed by what you and your wife desire.

Put another way, if things are acrimonious now, chances are they will be the same later without a solution to collaborate. Be fair to yourself and to the person you loved enough at one time and with whom you once considered spending your entire life.

This might be a lonely stance, but the payoff might be great if you accomplish it. Be the one to hold the big picture first, and open a discussion about what is truly important for everyone involved.

Here are some guiding questions for you to consider in the process and write in your journal:

✏️ JOURNAL ENTRY #212

What do you want your big picture to look like?

✏️ JOURNAL ENTRY #213

Are you open to asking your former spouse what her big picture is, and then collaborating to create a win-win?

✍ JOURNAL ENTRY #214

If you struggle to be open to this concept, what is in the way, and what's the next best thing you might choose?

✍ JOURNAL ENTRY #215

Whom might you ask to support you in this process?

Take Care of Yourself

During a divorce, many men often neglect themselves physically, nutritionally, emotionally, and spiritually. This is actually the time to do the exact opposite. Going through a divorce is a long, drawn-out process, and it takes more than a day, a week, a month, or even a year.

There are many emotional challenges along the way and some life-changing decisions to make. You need to be at your absolute best—even though you may feel at your worst. Stabilizing yourself in the areas of nutrition, rejuvenation, and exercise will support you in this process.

"Stabilization" means consciously choosing to maintain healthy standards in each of these areas. Keeping these areas stable may support you, so you may respond as resourcefully as possible to a challenging life situation. Nutritionally, this means you might pay attention to the quality of food you are feeding yourself. During an emotionally challenging process, such as a divorce, alcohol often does more harm than good. Consider reducing your intake or taking a sabbatical for a while.

"Rejuvenation" is all about doing something to restore you. This includes getting the rest you need, taking naps, getting massages, devoting some quiet time, or doing whatever you know makes you feel whole and complete. Make sure you are getting exercise and emotional support.

A divorce process is a marathon, so make sure you have the stamina to stay flexible, strong, and clear-headed.

Exercising (especially for men) is the easiest way to "get into your body," which is where your emotions reside. For most men, accessing and experiencing their emotions are challenging tasks—even if it is just to release their unconscious grip. Exercise actually helps relieve built-up anxiety and anger, and may even release some sadness.

I encourage you to find an exercising activity you enjoy and where you might meet other healthy people in the process. Many times during my divorce, I got on my bike feeling one way (with my head full of tangled thoughts) and finished my ride clear and unattached to what I had been thinking. I met other guys who were also maintaining themselves physically, and that was supportive as well.

Many men, who were athletic when they got married, often let themselves go physically as they struggled to find the balance of self-love and love for their family and work. You might think of taking care of yourself as an expression of self-love—an important prerequisite to being able to love others, which may serve you in your next relationship.

Now is a great time to master the elusive balance many men face, and being in better shape may help when you are ready to find another mate! Divorce is a highly stressful event that may go on for a long time. You may need to be in shape, and you may need your stamina.

Take the time, eliminate any distractions, and write down answers to the following questions in your journal:

✍ JOURNAL ENTRY #216

How would you assess your nutritional efforts? Do you eat balanced meals? On what areas might you improve?

JOURNAL ENTRY #217

How much alcohol are you drinking? Where might you cut back?

 JOURNAL ENTRY #218

What kind of things might you do for yourself to ensure feeling whole and rejuvenated?

 JOURNAL ENTRY #219

When was the last time you did something restorative for yourself?

 JOURNAL ENTRY #220

How in shape are you? Where might you improve your fitness level?

 JOURNAL ENTRY #221

What kind of exercise interests you? What sort of exercise do you enjoy doing?

Dating: Take It Low and Slow

One of the biggest mistakes men make when they are in the throes of divorce is to get into another relationship too soon, especially if a new relationship is being used to avoid the pain of looking at issues. It might be a mistake when the presence of the "new woman" confuses the kids.

More importantly, a new relationship may have a powerful effect on your soon-to-be former spouse. This, my friend, might be like adding a lit match to gasoline! A jealous or emotionally unstable woman in negotiations around finances and child custody might make for a less-than-stellar outcome—for everyone involved.

If I may, my suggestion is to take it "low and slow." Pay close attention to your needs, and watch for signs of escape or avoidance through involvement with another woman. There is nothing wrong with wanting to have a good time when you are going through a divorce. Just pay attention to *why* you are engaging other women, and stay aware of whether being in a relationship is wise for you at this time.

With that said, your "next woman" may have shown up in your life already. If this is the case (and you wish to proceed with awareness), I offer the following guidelines:

- Consider being friends and keeping things light for a while.

- Use the divorce process to gain insight about your behaviors in a relationship to avoid making the same mistake in your next relationship.

- Be aware of any desire to jump fully into another relationship, and stay on top of any desire to just "make it all go away."

- Consider the impact of "going public" with your new relationship as well as how your soon-to-be former spouse might receive it. Consider how this may negatively influence the divorce process.

- Only introduce a new woman to your kids if the relationship is serious, and consider taking it very slowly.

- Monitor the impact of a new woman on your children (and their adjustment to what is happening), and be aware of the effect of her presence on the success of your divorce process. Change her involvement, if necessary.

Navigating a divorce consciously is an inner game. If you recognize your emotions, manage them when they come up and be aware of how your emotions affect the people around you. This puts you "one leg up" on many other men.

You might find the acts of taking care of yourself during the divorce process and maintaining focus on coming to a win-win guide you and support your ability to work through the numerous decisions this process requires.

Remember: How you approach yourself and others during this difficult time will set the stage for how you interact later. There will be a later … a wonderful, healthy, moved-on-with-your-life later!

I promise.

CHAPTER 19

The Next Man

How can you encourage and support other men into being their "best man"?

It's Not Your Job to Change Your Friends

Your life is changing for the better, so it's natural to want your male friends to have the same experience you are having. In other words, you want them to wake up, too.

Maybe some of your friends have asked you direct questions about the changes you are making. Maybe you see your friends, colleagues, or neighbors struggling, oblivious to the impact they are creating in their relationships and in their lives. Of course, you feel the impulse to tell them what they may or might do.

Take my advice: *Avoid these impulses!*

After my men's weekend experience, I was so excited about waking up and getting to know myself that I made the mistake (on more than one occasion) of "encouraging" my guy friends to go to a men's weekend. However, what they heard was that "something is wrong with me," and they promptly ignored my invitation rather than hearing my genuine excitement for them.

After 13+ years of being on my path, I have learned that most men need a Volkswagen dropped on their head to get their attention. Life will hand you emotional pain, confusion, and chaos—with only the difficult path to choose—before you sit down, look at yourself, and make the necessary changes to be better. It is a rare man who sees the train wreck coming ahead of time, or pursues his personal growth in the absence of some massive internal pressure.

The saying, "A man knows when he is ready," means most men avoid change until *they decide they are ready.* All the convincing in the world is pointless to help them; they must *desire* to make a change.

So what are you supposed to do? The answer is "nothing" … initially.

You may first model for your friends, colleagues, and neighbors what it looks like to live your values, tell the truth, pursue emotionally literacy continuously, and, most of all, *stay conscious.* Acting from this place most certainly may stir the pot. You may find that, when *you* go there, you are inviting *them* to go there. When I have taken the risk to "be authentically me," most (if not all) of the men with whom I was interacting mirrored me (i.e., they imitated me).

If you lead, they will follow.

- If you find men who want to talk to you in depth about your learning and your path, gauge their level of openness to new things.

- Allow other men to drive the process.

- They might ask you to recommend books. If so, you may now recommend at least one!

- Feel free to mention your men's group or an initiatory men's weekend (assuming you attended one).

- If you witness other men in pain or being challenged in their life, ask them if they are interested in hearing what you did for yourself.

As a rule, avoid offering unsolicited advice. Men typically respond better when you share your welcomed experience.

Avoid your desire to "save" anyone and everyone. You may have an impact on an important man in your life, or on any man with whom you come in contact, by simply *being who you are*. I suggest you consider fully being who you are in all areas of your life because it will create a much richer experience in all you do.

You might use the "Guidelines to Becoming a Real Male Friend" (Chapter 17, "Real Male Friendships") to guide your encounters with men. Again, being a real male friend is not a precise science, and these guidelines may help you remember how to conduct yourself in a conscious way. These guidelines are about modeling for other men how you want them to be when they are with you. They help you *show* other men how to be and avoid *telling* them how to be.

You, This Book, and the Next Man

If your son, a best friend, a workmate, an employer, a client, or even a complete stranger asks you about this book, you might share why you picked it up and what you learned. I designed it to be a self-study book to allow each man to go at his own pace and learn how to ask for support.

Once I answered my wake-up call, participated in a men's weekend, and joined my own men's group, I became aware of how the vast majority of men whom I met in my life were unconscious and stuck in harmful patterns to themselves and to others. This was when I understood my responsibility as a man to do my part to change the world for the better.

I realized the best way to do this was by *being* the best man in all areas of my life, to lead by example, and to reach out to men when the occasion presented itself. Our children, spouses, communities, and planet might be much safer if more men wake up, step up, and man up.

The next male generation is waiting for you to show them how to do this, so feel free to reach out when the time is right. The opportunity to change the world for the better … one man at a time … is *now*.

CHAPTER 20

Final Words—My Story

E ver since my wake-up call in May 1999, I have been on a journey of personal discovery. Through this process, I've come to understand that who I am as a man is directly related to my many roles in life. Whether I'm being a father, a husband, a former husband, a male friend, a business partner, or a leader, I've learned that how I hold myself as a man matters and has a direct impact on those around me.

The disruption of my family and the pain of my divorce woke me up to this reality, and my wake-up call, while painful, changed my life. I might even say my wake-up call *started* my life—the one I was destined to live. Deeply within my core, I wanted to avoid going through life in a slumber, unaware, causing chaos in my relationships and experiences.

I resolved to set out on a healing journey, promising to stay awake and conscious to be a better man in all my life roles, especially as a co-parent with my former spouse. Little did I know this commitment would give birth to my life's purpose: supporting men on self-discovery journeys.

All kinds of men showed up on a regular basis 12 years ago, and they continue to show up in the following ways:

- I have shared various pieces of my life story with at least 2,000 men in an effort to let them know they have support during their wake-up call.

- I have drunk several hundred cups of coffee in intimate, one-on-one conversations with men in crisis or at crossroads in their lives.

- I have received hundreds upon hundreds of requests to sit down with somebody's husband, business partner, father, or son.

- I have encouraged 50+ men to sign up for a men's weekend. Some listened; many chose their own path.

I've brought my integrative whole-person style of coaching into the leadership and business arena, coaching chief executive officers, executives, and business professionals. I found that much of the business pains they were experiencing were rooted in their own personal pain. Bringing awareness and attention to this fact created significant internal shifts for them and their business.

On more than one occasion, I contemplated writing a book. Then, in one week, three different people told me I needed to write a book. Had I avoided writing this book, I might as well have been sitting on the bench instead of playing the game for which I had been preparing during thousands of hours of work. I realized and feared there might be consequences for other men if I failed to answer my call as God had intended.

In a morning meditation, the book inside me demanded I write it. Four months later, while navigating a career transition, I completed my book. I was running out of money, and it seemed like the absolute worst time to write a book—or was it the best time? My answer came when I was on a run with a friend and, as luck (or divine intervention) would have it, I landed hard on a rock and broke my foot.

The podiatrist told me I had to spend eight weeks in a walking boot—no running, cycling, or swimming. I was housebound. For an active guy like me, who usually spends 10-14 hours a week cycling and running, I might have easily gone into complaint and frustration mode. Instead, I took a different approach and said, "What perfect timing!"

Much to my surprise, I actually smiled inside and embraced my injury and lack of work as true gifts. Although my wife was concerned, and wanted to question my timing for writing this book, she gave me the support I needed. For that, I am grateful.

I chose to write this book because my mission is to inspire millions of men to answer their wake up-calls by becoming the men they are meant to me.

I realized that, no matter how much I wanted to help other men, one cup of coffee at a time was simply not scalable. Our country—hell, our *planet*—is in a Mandemic (a shortage of emotionally mature men who need to step up), so I decided to respond. If more men step into being better men in their roles as fathers, husbands, businessmen, leaders, and friends, then everyone wins.

Perhaps you resonate with some of my life struggles. Maybe my story might inspire you. If I turned my life around, reoriented it to my life's purpose, and then did something about it, *you might do the same thing*. I have shared my story hoping you may see yourself in mine. Better yet, I hope you see that you have the ability to rewrite your story as I have.

After my wake-up call, I floundered for a few months, unsure of whom to talk to or what I might do next. I was on a bike ride with a friend, who had been listening to me talk about my personal struggles and confusion.

"When you have an electrical or plumbing issue," my friend said, "you call an electrician or plumber. Go see a therapist."

Clearly, I was having some issues of the personal variety and some professional help might benefit me, so he offered a referral.

The therapist calmed me down and helped me gain some insight as to what was going on. I saw him for a while and felt good when I was in his office; however, once I went back to my life, it was the same—namely, *me*. I desired something more, and I was unsure of what "more" was. Communication with my former spouse was limited and I had to figure this out on my own ... or so I thought.

A month or so later, I was having an office meeting with my partner Alex, and my manager Kris walked in, obviously upset. He had just gotten off the phone with our syndicate desk and learned that I had yelled at the guy on the other end of the line when I didn't get my way.

"Sometimes you act so out of control," Kris told me. "You've got to get a handle on yourself!"

After Kris closed the door behind him, Alex turned to me.

"Ray, I don't get you. Sometimes you act with a huge sense of entitlement."

Wow! That was two piercing statements inside of five minutes. I knew they were both right and something inside me stirred.

"I have heard this before," I thought, "from my wife, her best friend, and now at work."

I knew something had to change. I walked into Kris's office and asked if he had a moment. Surprisingly, I thanked him for what he said and apologized for putting him in a compromising position. I told him I needed and wanted to change, and I was struggling to know what to do.

Kris told me to close the door and have a seat. He reached into his bureau and pulled out a brochure for a men's weekend event called the New Warrior Adventure Training. Kris smiled and looked me in the eye.

"If you are willing to check your shit at the door, Ray, this weekend is for you. I can't tell you what goes on there, but I can tell you that it changed my life. You can call my wife and ask her."

My marriage was in shambles and my career had hit a major bump. These two events conspired to give me the one-two punch to which I was determined to respond. I was ready to attend a men's initiation weekend, and the next one was a whole four months away. I wanted one now, so I made the decision to get on a plane to Houston.

I went to Houston to attend the New Warrior Adventure Training with the intention to fix my marriage. Within two hours of being at the weekend event, I realized that, if any fixing needed to happen, it was going to start with me. I was the problem with my marriage. It really wasn't even about fixing me; it was about healing and growing personally and becoming the man I was destined to be.

For the first time in my life, I was with a group of powerful, articulate, emotionally literate men, who were on a path to be the best men possible. They were fathers, grandfathers, sons, brothers, leaders, gay and straight, and multicultural. I had an extremely powerful weekend and flew back a new man.

I actually felt like a man.

While I had a powerful and life-changing weekend, life at home was exactly as I left it, and I was now better equipped to handle it. At the weekend, I connected to my vitality and learned about authenticity, honor, integrity, and accountability. These were now my masculine core values, and I would need to access them regularly to guide my behaviors and decisions. I would also have a core support group of men, who were all on similar paths and who would constantly challenge me to be better.

My first real test came with my impending divorce. My wife and I were choosing separate paths. Despite my efforts to attend the men's weekend, join a weekly men's group, and read a bunch of books, I had to deal with the very real, hard truth: I was going to go through a divorce.

Much of what I say about navigating conscious divorce comes from my own experience. I hired a relationship specialist to help us get through our divorce as thoughtfully and consciously as possible. To this day, my former wife and I have a good relationship as co-parents because we worked together to set things up that way. It was difficult and I say honestly, I have few regrets.

Hard personal work as a single father ensued after the divorce. Then, I had the wonderful opportunity to meet and fall in love with my soul mate Anna, who is now my wife. More than anything, I wanted a second chance to be in an intimate relationship with a woman where I could bring all of who I am as a man.

I recall telling myself that I wanted to meet a woman who would be a great step-mom to my kids, who would avoid being offended or triggered by my functioning relationship with my former wife, and who might be willing to look at her own self in the spirit of growing our relationship together.

I had met Anna 20 years prior when we were in our twenties. While our first lunch date as young adults was premature for our eventual relationship, our second go around was for keeps.

Saying that I've been a perfect man or a perfect husband to Anna is far from the truth. During the course of our marriage, I have staffed over 30 men's weekends, attended a Healing the Mother Wound workshop, staffed a men's training inside Folsom Prison, and attended countless other workshops and trainings. After each one, I came home to my wife, seeking to be better with her in some way. My work as a man, a husband, a father, and a leader continues.

My three children, now teenagers, have been my teachers in many ways. They have all challenged me and, in each child, I see parts of myself. My courageous daughter, who is 19 years old, recently completed 30 days in an inpatient facility for an eating disorder. She has embraced her recovery and is now on her way to inspire other young people with eating disorders as she navigates her college experience. My two boys, ages 17 and 14, are currently at the center of my attention while I assist them on their path to becoming responsible young men. Both of them have attended a rite of passage weekend for young men.

In 2004, I met my friend John, who has taught me a lot about being in an authentic and truthful relationship with another man. We've had some discord, shared tears, and had a ton of fun. Our relationship has stretched me and I have grown. I have subsequently established deeper, more supportive relationships with several other men. I can't imagine my life without them.

In February 2007, I took a leap of faith to follow my truth path and left the financial services business and the money that went along with it. Little did I know my career transition would last more than five years and how much it would challenge me, teach me, and grow me on a personal level.

I have had several exciting possibilities followed by nothing. I have gotten glimmers and glimpses of what is possible, but my "big break" has not happened yet. The big learning for me is that *it is my responsibility to make my big break happen.*

Here is what I know: I am stepping fully into my gifts and bringing them into the world. I'm always marching forward. I am building my dream existence, one brick at a time, and forever learning in the process.

It's all about faith, patience, confidence, perseverance, and intuition.

I intend to write another book about navigating this transition from work life to life's work. I intend to write this next book to inspire others and help them break the journey into bite-size chunks to make the task less daunting.

Maybe you are contemplating a big change like I have. When I complete my entrepreneurial journey and figure out how this works, I'll definitely let you know. You can expect an invitation and a guidebook!

Wanna join me?

CHAPTER 21

Note to Women

W hen I decided to write a book for men, it occurred to me that the audience I needed to include and speak to were women—especially women who are in relationship with men.

Since women are more apt to buy self-help books and have a vested interest in a man journeying inward, it made sense to address this right off the bat. My hope is that this brief section sheds light on the possibilities for you and him amidst his wake-up call, if he chooses to answer it.

I wrote this section for women with three potential scenarios in mind:

First, you might be in a relationship with a man who is in the midst of his wake-up call. I wanted to provide an overview of what this means to you, of what your role is, and what you can expect.

Second, you might be in a relationship with a man who is going through a "man crisis" of sorts. I wanted to provide a way for both of you to understand what is going on for him and to provide you with the opportunity to give him this book as a gesture of support.

Third, you might be in the midst of your own wake-up call about your relationship with him. You may have recently woken up to the reality that something has to change in your relationship with him, or you are leaving (and you mean it). How you share this information with him can have the equivalent effect of creating his wake-up call. You can use leverage to encourage your man to go on his men's journey. Depending on your circumstances, this could save and possibly improve your relationship.

You will need to be willing to answer your own wake-up call and go on your woman's journey as well. After I wrote this book, I realized that women could also experience a wake-up call of sorts in their relationship with their man. You can contact me for coaching or feel free to use this book and its Roadmaps for your situation, recognizing that many of the principles slanted towards men will work for you.

Maybe the man about whom you are concerned is a boyfriend or a husband. Maybe he is an ex-husband (or on his way to being one, if he doesn't get his act together). Maybe he is your brother or even your dad. He might be just a friend. Regardless of who this man is, he is lucky to have you in his life because you care.

You and Your Role

I would like to take a moment and acknowledge what may be going on with you before I discuss—and offer suggestions—about what's going on with your man.

You may be worried about your man's emotional, physical, or even spiritual well-being. You may be worried about your own well-being. You may be wondering if he loves you. You may not feel safe with him anymore. You may have emotionally moved on (or are quite close to moving on) and are at the stage of last resort. Maybe the kids have left the nest and it's a whole new ball game.

Whatever is happening for you as a woman, this book offers an easy way to support your man. You aren't asking him to go to therapy. You aren't asking him to go to a workshop or hire a coach. You're just asking him to read a book.

If you do it with love (including self-love), this gesture can communicate three things:

1. It will let him know that you care.
2. It will tell him that nothing is wrong with him.
3. It will show that he is not alone in what's going on for him.

If you give this book to him under challenging emotional circumstances in your relationship with him, you can use the leverage of a wavering relationship as an incentive for him to read the book and start his journey.

Your role, for now, is the loving messenger ... loving yourself (and him) enough to take a risk and give him this book. It may be your—and his—last resort.

What's Up with Him?

This man, whom you know and love, is in a tunnel—a "nonstage" of life—where everything that was working for him may not be working anymore. He is not yet aware of his part in creating his wake-up call. He is uncomfortable and possibly in emotional pain.

What was interesting to him no longer holds his interest, and he's probably feeling disoriented. His career may no longer excite him. His father or mother may have died. His friend, or even he, may have had a health scare. You might have left him. He might have left himself. He is experiencing feelings that he doesn't know how to understand, and he honestly doesn't know what to do. He has yet to comprehend that a new way of being a man is the only way he can advance.

It is likely that this man hasn't had much training about his feelings. He may not have had a good role model for what it means to be a man in today's world. Because of this fact, it is a double whammy: He is experiencing feelings that he doesn't know how to understand, and the number of people to whom he can talk and from whom he can get support is limited because his nomadic macho training has always been, "Do not ask for help."

He is in a place where he has many more questions than answers, and he is in a bind. He can't come to you (yet) because he really doesn't know himself.

You are not a man … you are a woman. In other words, he can't come to a woman for advice about a "man transition." He needs to go to other men who have experienced this journey in their lives.

What Can You Do or Say?

While you may be inclined to support him in a variety of ways, the best thing you can do now is understand where he is. He is in a place that contains confusion, sadness, boredom, aloneness, anger, fear, shame, and ego (both survival ego and pointless ego). Men will endure this mixture of emotions for a very long time until they reach a point of desperation and become willing to do just about anything.

This moment can be quite tricky. Your man is not at his best, and is most certainly not in his grounded masculine power. For most women, seeing a man in this state can make them feel worried and unsafe.

It may be best for you to put some healthy distance between you and your man as he figures out his path. The key is to communicate that this distance is not a punitive move but instead a mutual honor of each other's processes. Let him know that you understand this difficult time and that his best form of support may be from men. Let him know that you aren't going away (if you are still in a relationship with him).

If you are still in his life, and you have his attention and possibly his respect, use loving leverage and give him this book.

What's In It for You?

If your man reads this book and does each exercise contained in its pages, different things could happen. You just might get a real man back—a man who does what he says and honors his commitments. You might get a man who is grounded and more aware. You might get a man who is more mindful, more loving, present, and surer of himself. Depending on who your man is, you might get all of this and much more.

It's OK to Want Something Back

Remember that it's OK to want the best from your man. Maybe you want the guy you fell in love with to walk back in the door. Maybe you want the best father possible for the kids you have with him, whether you stay with him or not. Maybe you see him struggling and want the best for him because you care. You might want more peace in your life because, if there isn't enough in his, there won't be enough in yours.

Whatever you want, it's OK to want it, and wanting something better for your man is a good thing. Deep inside, this man also wants to be better, and there is a lot of confidence that a man can carry on his journey when he knows his woman is rooting for him.

I designed this book to meet each man where he is, and give him guidance to get answers for which he is so desperately looking. If your man reads and works through this book, you may see him start to re-evaluate more consciously how he shows up in his relationship with you.

I will ask him to understand the influences his father and mother had on him, and think about how those influences play out in his relationships that may include you. The central positive thrust of this book is to encourage each man to answer his wake-up call and identify how he can be a better man in the various roles in his life.

Be patient, encourage him along the way, and don't rescue him. If he follows the instructions in this book, he will do his emotional work in the company of other men. Then, when he shows up again in your life, he will look and act more like the man you always wanted and knew he could be.

Resources

Menstuff.org

I can direct many of the references in this book to Menstuff.org. I choose (and use) this resource because I am a big believer in *not* reinventing the wheel. I personally know and have a relationship with the founder, Gordon Clay, and can vouch for his passion in the world of men's work. His website is quite abundant, and it is fair to say that it's a book of books in and of itself!

This educational website is the starting point for information for and about men. Menstuff serves a diverse men's community, and deals with men's rights, mytho-poetic issues, profeminist subjects, recovery, re-evaluation counseling, and spiritual matters.

Menstuff has 65 columnists reporting on a weekly or monthly basis. The website lists thousands of on-site men's book reviews and covers, men's resources and hyperlinks, and hundreds of events, periodicals, and groups. It provides information on many men's issues regarding positive change in male roles and relationships, including abuse, aging, circumcision, divorce, fathers, health, kids' stuff, mid-life topics, multi-cultural challenges, prostate cancer, relationships, sexuality, spirituality, testicular cancer, violence, and work.

Menstuff always provides the original source of their material; however, as weeks, months, or years go by, many of those sources end. If it weren't for Menstuff.org, much of that information would be lost forever. Therefore, if you find a broken link, realize that this is probably what happened. They leave the broken link there so you know the original source of the information.

On Menstuff.org, you will also find links to quite an assortment of men's groups that can go a long way in supporting you—especially with the first Roadmap step (Chapter 4, "Roadmap Step #1—Create Support for Yourself").

My Experience with Specific Programs

I mention other references in this book because I experienced them and they were helpful for me or for someone I know. I cannot guarantee that you will have the same takeaways, yet I have confidence that you will have your own rich experience.

Men's Initiation Weekend

The ManKind Project®: New Warrior Training Adventure

mankindproject.org

I had my initiatory experience with The ManKind Project (MKP), a global not-for-profit organization (501(c)(3) in the United States) that conducts challenging and highly rewarding training for men at every stage of life. They help men through any transition, at all levels of success, and while facing almost any challenge.

Their flagship training, described by many as the most powerful men's training available, is the New Warrior Training Adventure. The MKP is not affiliated with any religious practice or political party. Your beliefs are welcome. They strive to be inclusive and affirming of cultural differences, especially with respect to color, class, sexual orientation, faith, age, ability, ethnicity, and nationality.

Other Initiation Weekends

Other men's organizations that provide initiation trainings are available at Menstuff.org. You can search under men's retreats and workshops.

Young Men's Ultimate Weekend

www.ymuw.org

This experiential weekend is for young men ages 13–20. Both of my sons have attended this weekend and I was very impressed with the program, what my boys experienced, and how they showed up in our home.

The Young Men's Ultimate Weekend was founded by Dr. Mark Shillinger in 2000. The mission of the weekend is to mentor young men to live life with integrity, to give and get respect, to master their energy, and to interact with their family and community by modeling honorable, confident behaviors so they can become responsible and moral adults.

Understanding Women

PAX Workshop: Understanding Women: Unlock the Mystery™
www.understandmen.com/understandingwomen/index.html

Allison Armstrong, author of several books and the founder of the PAX workshops, has developed an amazing and insightful workshop for men and women to experience in each of their respective pursuits to understand women. Whether it is for your spouse, your daughter, or business peers, having an in-depth understanding of the women in your life is the key to more fun, intimate, and satisfying relationships. With the unique perspective and information this workshop offers, you can transform your frustrations into opportunities for compassion, humor, and effective resolutions.

I attended this workshop in 2011 and it was a fantastic experience. I walked away with many new tools and perspectives I was able to use in my personal and professional relationships.

Understanding Women: Unlock the Mystery is for anyone who wants to understand why women do what they do—how they think, act, speak, and listen—and learn how to work with these traits instead of being frustrated by them!

Silent Meditation Retreat and Emotional Koan Work

Mondo Zen: Hollow Bones Retreats

www.mondozen.org

I attended this seven-day sesshin and it changed my life. I learned about meditation and ways to work with my anger and shame. This primary influence assisted me in curtailing my anger outbursts in my marriage and while parenting. I participated in an all-male group where each man had attended the New Warrior Training Adventure (see "The ManKind Project: New Warrior Training Adventure," above).

Hollow Bones Zen retreats, now called Mondo Zen Sesshin, are a modern adaptation of the traditional Japanese Rinzai Zen retreats. All practices during the seven- and three-day retreats offered by Hollow Bones are done in English in order to facilitate direct, personal understanding of the methods and goals. In addition to traditional Zazen (sitting meditation) and Koan study, Yoga or Internal Martial Arts is part of the daily practice.

In this school of Zen, it is essential that you awaken, and there is a fierce, yet compassionate, insistence that you do so now. Meditating and sitting quietly is not enough! You must realize your inherent freedom. You must answer the question, "Who are you?" from the purest depths of realization, moving far beyond the normal modes of speculative thought.

The Hollow Bones retreats offer men and women the opportunity to experience the "answer" to this question in a way that transcends all hope, fear, and doubt. Their retreats are co-ed unless specifically described on the booking page.

Healing the Mother Wound® Workshop

www.fatherwound.com/motherwound.html

I attended this workshop in 2004 and, without a doubt, it changed how I related to my wife. I learned about my relationship with my mother and how it was affecting my marriage, how it contributed to my divorce, and how—if I wasn't careful—I would model for my sons how to incorrectly interact with the women in their life.

I was able to heighten my awareness around my behaviors in my marriage and improve our relationship as a result. This workshop was extremely powerful given that I had a significant mother wound. I participated in this workshop with 12 men and found it to be healing and liberating.

The workshop confronts your old patterns, beliefs, and stuffed emotions around your mother. Through your navel, you have the visible evidence of your link to your biological mother—a link encoded with messages, such as your history, patterns, destiny, and even your sense of self. You inherit your self-worth from your mother. You are tied to the woman who birthed you, and you are tied to the generations that preceded you.

In this workshop, you delve into mythology, archetypes, and shadow aspects. You examine the power of the dark feminine, and the regenerative nature of the creator/destroyer. You explore how you project what you don't want to acknowledge in yourself onto others. You came into this world through your mother's body. You have a purpose. When you can come out from under the shroud of shame, anger, resentment, fear, and isolation, you can be free to live your soul's purpose.

My Programs

My intention around bringing forth programs by my design is about serving and addressing a need or needs that may be unmet as of the printing of this book. I offer the following and I encourage you to go to www.yourmensjourney.com.

Continuity Program

This low-priced membership program offers regular and helpful insights, suggestions, videos, and the opportunity to connect with other men on their men's journey. Go to www.yourmensjourney.com for further details.

Online Group Coaching Program

Online programs are in development for you to put the Roadmap steps in this book into action with the support of other men on their men's journey. Go to www.yourmensjourney.com for further details.

Individual "Break Through" Coaching

I offer a comprehensive, intensive, high-cost/high-touch, one-on-one, 90-day coaching program for a limited number of qualified people. You can find more details at rayarata.com

Mastermind Gatherings

Come to these all-male gathering of other fellow course graduates in a natural outdoor setting that includes physical activities to support the curriculum.

CPSIA information can be obtained
at www.ICGtesting.com
Printed in the USA
FFOW02n1747040314
4038FF